Lizards Rare & Common
Tom Mazorlig

Chamaeleo pardalis. Photo: Marian Bacon

© T.F.H. Publications, Inc.

Distributed in the UNITED STATES to the Pet Trade by T.F.H. Publications, Inc., 1 TFH Plaza, Neptune City, NJ 07753; on the Internet at www.tfh.com; in CANADA by Rolf C. Hagen Inc., 3225 Sartelon St., Montreal, Quebec H4R 1E8; Pet Trade by H & L Pet Supplies Inc., 27 Kingston Crescent, Kitchener, Ontario N2B 2T6; in ENGLAND by T.F.H. Publications, PO Box 74, Havant PO9 5TT; in AUSTRALIA AND THE SOUTH PACIFIC by T.F.H. (Australia), Pty. Ltd., Box 149, Brookvale 2100 N.S.W., Australia; in NEW ZEALAND by Brooklands Aquarium Ltd., 5 McGiven Drive, New Plymouth, RD1 New Zealand; in SOUTH AFRICA by Rolf C. Hagen S.A. (PTY.) LTD., P.O. Box 201199, Durban North 4016, South Africa; in JAPAN by T.F.H. Publications. Published by T.F.H. Publications, Inc.
MANUFACTURED IN THE
UNITED STATES OF AMERICA
BY T.F.H. PUBLICATIONS, INC.

Contents

Adult female *Iguana iguana*. Photo: Candi Foltz

BASIC CARE & FEEDING

INTRODUCTION

Lizards are fascinating. Many are pretty and some are just plain cool, but if you are reading this book you probably know that. Hopefully, you also know that to live long, healthy, happy lives in captivity, lizards must have all of their needs provided for them by the keeper. The purpose of this book is to introduce you to many types of lizards and their care and to help you decide which lizard (or lizards) is the right one for you. Different species of lizards obviously require different types of housing and food, different basking temperatures, and so on, and not every hobbyist can provide for the needs of every lizard. Once you read this book you should be able to select a lizard that will fit into your budget, lifestyle, and idea of the type of pet—owner relationship you desire (i.e., whether it is more important that your lizard be a tame pet or just be an interesting and attractive animal to observe and care for). If you already own a lizard or lizards, this book will introduce you to some other types that may spark your interest and perhaps may tell you a thing or two you didn't know about the species you keep.

My interest in lizards (and reptiles and other animals in general) has been long-standing. As a young boy I was enchanted by the small Green Anoles in pet stores as

A "designer" Leopard Gecko, *Eublepharis macularius*, is a result of increased captive-breeding of this and many other species of lizards. Photo: G. & C. Merker

they leapt from branch to branch and snatched up mealworms with a dinosaur-like ferocity. As a boy I kept many lizards, from anoles to chameleons to tegus—unsuccessfully. I learned the hard way that lizards cannot be expected to thrive when given only a cage and some crickets, which is what pet stores and books often said at the time. Now I keep and breed several species, along with snakes and a tortoise. It is my hope that you will not have to go through the same casualties that I did. Since the days of my youth, herpetoculture (the keeping and breeding of reptiles and amphibians in captivity) has become a more mainstream hobby, and information on these animals has become easier to find. Today's new and young hobbyists reap the rewards of knowledge gained from mistakes made by myself and my peers. Take advantage of that. This book is meant as an introduction, not the final word. After reading this and acquiring a lizard or three, dig deeper into the literature for more information on the species you keep. Talk to other keepers and breeders and share the expertise you develop. Strive to be a better keeper, a better breeder. Your animals will reward you with good health, robust babies, and a sense of wonder and accomplishment.

THE IMPORTANCE OF THERMOREGULATION

It is a widely held belief that lizards are cold-blooded. Many of you may know that this is not exactly true. What is true is that lizards do not produce heat through their metabolism but depend upon the environment around them to provide it. Each species of lizard has its own range of body temperatures that are best for normal behavior, digestion, reproduction, and the other functions of life. This does not necessarily mean that if the temperature of the environment falls out of the optimal range the lizard will die. There is a range outside the optimal range that includes survivable temperatures. These aren't the best for the lizard and if kept in such temperatures for long enough death might ensue, but the lizard can tolerate them for periods of time. Although geared toward lizards, most of this section applies to other reptiles as well and, to some extent, amphibians.

If a lizard depends on the outside environment for its heat, how does it keep its body temperature in the optimal or at least acceptable range? Lizards do this with a set of behaviors, therefore the regulation of temperature—thermoregulation—by lizards is called behavioral thermoregulation. Many different behaviors may be used, each depending on the species and its environment. The basic idea is that a lizard will move to a warm area to heat itself up and move to a cooler area to cool itself down. For Bearded Dragons, Green Iguanas, and many others, this often means moving to a patch of sunlight and basking until they get sufficiently hot (optimal body core temperature), then moving off to forage, mate, or just cool down in the shade. Other lizards, like many nocturnal geckos, will warm up by lying on rocks that were heated by the sun during the day. Not surprisingly, most night-active lizards prefer lower temperatures than day-active ones. Burrowing lizards often warm themselves by burrowing under a sun-warmed rock or patch of ground. The heat passes through the rocks to their bodies.

What does all this mean for the lizard-keeper? Well, to start with, it means you must know the temperature range your lizard does best at and provide it. It also means that just heating your lizard is not enough; you must provide the animal with a range of temperatures so that it may regulate its own body temperature through behavior; this range of temperatures is called a thermal gradient. Don't be discouraged; it isn't as difficult to do this as it may sound. You will need *multiple* thermometers to measure the temperature at the hot and cold ends of the cage, and you should also measure the temp at the hottest basking spot.

A number of different heating devices may be employed, together or by themselves, to keep your lizard's cage in the proper range. The key to providing a proper thermal gradient to your pet is to have a large enough cage with all of the heating equipment at one end of it. This means one end will be nice and toasty, holding a temperature at or above the high end of the lizard's optimal zone. The other end will be substantially cooler, and there will be a gentle cline from one end to the other.

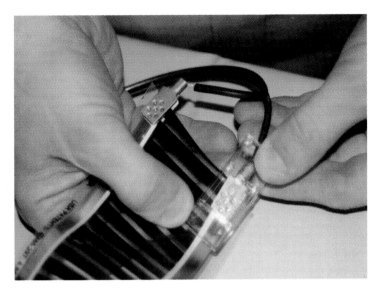

Heat tapes are just one of many types of heaters that can be used in lizard enclosures. No matter what type of heater is used, it should be designed to produce the proper thermal gradient for the pet. Photo: M. Walls

them only in ceramic-based sockets—they will melt plastic ones and start a fire), and night lights (blue or red lights that don't affect lizard—or human—sleep cycles) can be used. Heat rocks are not recommended as they warm up one small area. This often means the rest of the cage is too cold, so the lizard sits on the rock all of the time and burns itself. When using any and all heat devices, make sure they do not get hot enough to burn the lizard and that the lizard cannot get into direct contact with bulbs.

In the sections on individual lizards, the temperature ranges and methods of providing them will be discussed in more detail.

LIGHTING DOES MORE THAN JUST ILLUMINATE

For lizards, light has several functions. One of the major ones, providing heat, was mentioned above. The other very obvious one is that

Most commonly, heat lamps are the heat sources used. These are excellent because they provide light along with heat. By trying bulbs of different wattages, you should be able to find one that keeps the cage properly warm. Sometimes more than one light may be needed. Undertank heaters can be used alone on glass aquariums housing lizards that prefer moderate heat, or along with a light to provide higher temperatures for those lizards that require them. Remember that the natural behavior of the lizard will determine what heat sources you use; undertank heaters are next to useless for chameleons and other arboreal species.

Another important point is that most lizards prefer that the temperature drop a number of degrees at night (the exact drop depending on the species in question). This means shutting off some of your heating devices. You may

not want to shut off all of the heaters, since some lizards still need a temperature above the normal room temperature even during the night. To supply this, undertank heaters, ceramic heat emitters (devices that screw into light bulb sockets and generate heat but no visible light; use

Though widely available and easy to use, hot rocks can be dangerous for some species, providing heat only from below that could result in serious burns. Their heat also is very localized within the enclosure, not producing a gradient. Photo: M. Walls

it allows them (and the humans viewing them) to see. These two things are tremendously important in and of themselves. However, light has even more roles in the life of a lizard.

One of the functions of light is to provide a sense of time, of day and night and the changing of seasons. This may not seem terribly important until you consider this example: How happy would you be if you were kept in a well-lit environment all of the time? How happy would you be if you were kept in a dark environment all of the time? A lizard wouldn't like it either. Therefore, you should use lights to provide a day/night cycle, called a photoperiod. Photoperiod is usually expressed in shorthand as the hours of light vs. the hours of darkness, like this: 14:10. In this example, there are 14 hours of light and 10 of darkness, making a full 24-hour day. Most lizards will do well if allowed 12 to 14 hours of light per day. Some, such as nocturnal species, would prefer less, and a few, mostly equatorial species, would like more. It is true that the

incidental sunlight from the windows will help give your lizards a day and night, but artificial lighting is invaluable if you intend to manipulate the hours of light over the course of time, such as when attempting breeding, or if you wish to give them longer days than your area is currently receiving. The photoperiod should not be varied randomly or changed quickly. Changes should be made gradually. If you change the photoperiod suddenly, or if you do not give your lizards a regular photoperiod, they sometimes exhibit odd behaviors, become withdrawn, or become aggressive. It is easier to control the amount of light your lizards receive if you use a timer.

The last function of light a lizard keeper has to concern him/herself with is nutrition. It may come as a surprise to some of you that light affects nutrition, but it does. Specifically, one type of light, the ultraviolet-B waves (UV-B), reacts with a chemical in the skin of many animals (lizards, turtles, and humans to name only a few), producing vitamin D. Vitamin D plays a role in calcium

metabolism, allowing the body to absorb the mineral through the digestive tract. When there is a shortage of vitamin D, an animal develops skeletal abnormalities including enlarged, fragile, and misshapen bones. In nature, lizards get their UV-B from sunlight. Basking serves not only to heat a lizard but also to provide it with adequate levels of vitamin D.

Many lizards seem to need access to UV-B for normal development of the skeleton. Others seem to do just fine when they consume adequate levels of vitamin D in the diet. As a good generality, if the lizard you are keeping basks heavily in the wild or is otherwise exposed to intense levels of sunlight, it probably will do best if you provide it with UV-B. Nocturnal lizards, of course, do not need UV-B.

There are two major ways to provide UV-B to your lizards. The most obvious one is sunlight. I strongly encourage you to give your basking lizards access to natural sunlight. However, you must be careful not to overheat them. Glass cages should never be set in the sun. They heat up very quickly, and lizards inside them will die if not rescued in time. Additionally, glass filters out a large percentage of ultraviolet light, meaning that the light coming through a glass cage or a window is not going to do your pet any good. The sunlight has to be unfiltered through glass. This usually means having your lizard in some type of screen or mesh enclosure when it is put out into the sun. If you have a secure and safe screened-in porch, you can let

The right lights could make all the difference in the appearance and behavior of your pet. Basking lizards need the proper amount of UV-B each day. Photo courtesy of Energy Savers Unlimited, Inc.

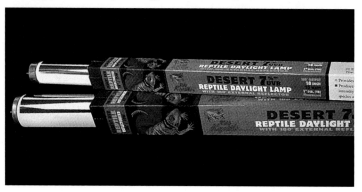

your lizard out onto the porch for sunlight. (I used to let my chameleons roam in the collection of houseplants that hung on our porch in the summer.) Even if you have a screen cage to take your lizard out for some sun, it still will overheat if you do not provide shade. Roughly half of the cage should be shaded, and adequate drinking water provided. Check the cage periodically, as the sun moves over the course of the day. At 10 AM, half the cage might be in the shade, but perhaps at 1 PM the entire enclosure will be bathed in sunlight. As long as you are cautious, taking your lizard out in the sun is of great benefit.

Unfortunately, most of us do not live in areas where the weather allows us to house our lizards outdoors or to take them outside several times weekly. If that is the case, you must rely on the second method of providing UV-B to your lizards: full-spectrum lighting. These fluorescent bulbs emit light that is as nearly similar to sunlight as can currently be made. Plant bulbs are not the same and generally do not produce sufficient UV-B. There are many varieties of full-spectrum bulbs on the market, but it is best to use one that was made specifically for reptiles. Most pet stores now carry these. These bulbs are only effective if your lizard can position itself less than 12 inches from the bulb and if the bulb is replaced at least yearly. When using full-spectrum lights, make sure there are shaded areas in the enclosure so the lizards can escape the light if they desire. It has been suggested that

some desert lizards and others that bask heavily do best when there is more than one full-spectrum bulb shining into the cage. Remember that glass filters out ultraviolet, meaning that a glass cage top will render your expensive bulb useless.

FEEDING BASICS

It is often said that you are what you eat. There is some truth to this adage. An unhealthy diet makes for an unhealthy animal—whether that animal is a human, a crayfish, or a lizard is immaterial. This chapter will give you the basic information on how to compose your lizard's diet, while the section on the specific lizard you keep will provide the details.

Too often I've heard pet store workers and reptile show vendors answer the question "What do I feed it?" by saying "Just feed it crickets," or "Just feed it mice." Almost no lizard is going to be in the best condition if you buy crickets or mice from a pet store and just toss them into the cage.

There's quite a bit more to it than that.

In general, most lizards in the hobby are insectivores. Many are carnivores (which almost always start out as insectivores when young) or omnivores, and a small percentage are herbivores. This section will discuss the insectivores and carnivores, leaving the description of the lizard in question to fill out the diet for the rest of the saurians. Also remember that most lizards require that clean, fresh water be available all the time.

INSECTIVORES

Insectivorous lizards are the majority of lizards in the hobby. This group includes almost all the geckos, almost all the chameleons, the anoles, the swifts, smaller monitors, whiptails, and many more. In nature, most species eat a wide variety of insects, worms, spiders, and other invertebrates. Larger forms will take the occasional vertebrate when the opportunity presents itself. Most of the time, the

The domestic cricket, *Acheta domesticus,* is an excellent staple in the diet of most lizards, but it should never be fed without supplementation or as the only food. All lizards need variety in their diets. Photo: A. Norman

invertebrates that the lizards consume are themselves well-fed and might even have a belly full of food. They are literally packed with nutrients for the lizard to digest. In a captive situation, if you are just dumping freshly purchased crickets or mealworms into the cage you have an entirely different scenario. The crickets and mealworms from the store usually have not been fed any form of nutritious diet. If they have been fed at all, they were probably only given some chunks of apples or potatoes. In short, they have been nutrient depleted. To feed these invertebrate bags of water and fiber to your lizard and then expect your lizard to thrive is unrealistic. The lizard has evolved to feed on a wide variety of nutritious insects; your captive will not do well if given one or two types of nutrient-poor insects.

Solving this problem takes a multifaceted approach. One part of the solution is to feed the food. When you purchase feeder insects, don't feed them to your lizards right away.

Feed the insects first. The most commonly purchased insects, crickets and mealworms, are easy to feed.

Put your crickets in a ventilated container of some sort. Give them some crumpled newspaper, paper towel tubes, or pieces of egg crates to hide in (without these, crickets tend to trample and kill each other). Crickets eat just about anything, so it's easy to load them up on nutritious food. You can use commercial cricket diets, bread, crushed non-sugar cereals, wheat bran, tropical fish food, rabbit pellets, oatmeal, or any other inexpensive grainy food. This is the base food. I mix it with a small amount of vitamin/mineral powder. To provide the insects with water and some extra nutrition, include a few pieces of one or more of the following: sweet potatoes, carrots, squash, zucchini, broccoli stems, leafy green vegetables (kale, collards, endive, etc.), oranges, or green beans. After 24 to 48 hours of feeding on these items, the nutrient value of the crickets

has increased tremendously, making them a better food for your lizards. Mealworms are even simpler to feed. Put them in a container that has been filled to a depth of 1 to 2 inches with wheat bran, oatmeal, whole wheat flour, and/or crushed non-sugar cereals (again, I mix this with some vitamin/mineral powder). Lay some pieces of vegetable on top. On top of this add some crumpled paper; the mealworms will crawl up into it and collect there, making it easy to find them at feeding time. The mealworms will even breed in such circumstances (except for the king or super mealworms; these are rather difficult to breed for the average hobbyist), so you will have a renewable food supply.

Feeding the food is only part of the answer. Variety is another part. Try to cycle different insects into the diet of your lizards. Crickets make a fine staple for most insectivores, but it is important to give them other items often. Aside from crickets and mealworms, many pet stores carry waxworms, small, maggot-like caterpillars. While these are not the most nutritionally rich insects, they add variety to the diet and are high in fats, making them a good choice for putting some weight on skinny animals or females that just laid eggs. Some pet stores carry flightless fruitflies and flightless houseflies. The former are great for hatchlings and tiny lizards, and the latter are relished by many arboreal lizards. For large insectivores, such as Veiled Chameleons and Bearded Dragons, you can try

Next to crickets, mealworms (Tenebrio molitor larvae) are perhaps the most commonly fed live food for lizards. Photo: M. Smith

Drosophila hydei, **the "giant" fruitfly, is an easily cultured and fed food that is great for geckos and other small insectivores.** Photo: M. Walls

Snakes. So, avoid collecting these types. Other than those simple guidelines, go forth and collect. Flies, moths, and butterflies can be caught with nets. Turning over logs and rocks often reveals pillbugs, beetles, and other critters. Spiders are relished by many lizards. Most lizards avoid eating ants, but you can try a few and see. Feed out wild-collected insects right away so they don't lose their nutritious gut contents.

SUPPLEMENTATION

In your ongoing efforts to give your lizards the best diet possible, there are two more facets to discuss: gut-loading and vitamin dusting. Gut-loading is an extension of feeding your insects. The difference is that you are feeding them a high vitamin and mineral diet before giving them to your lizards. Set up your crickets as you would normally, but the food will be somewhat different. Mix equal portions of vitamin/mineral supplements and the oatmeal,

the giant hissing cockroaches often sold as pets. These make expensive food, so if you keep larger lizards you may want to look into breeding them yourself. By checking reptile magazines, reptile shows, and the Internet, you may find suppliers of other insects. Recently, silkworms have become available. These are highly nutritious items, though they are hard to keep.

Collecting insects from the wild is a wonderful option, as it gives your lizards some variety and nutrition and gets you outdoors and active as well. Before collecting wild insects, there are some things to keep in mind. First, make sure you collect from an area that is not sprayed with pesticides, fungicides, chemical fertilizers, etc. Many public lands are sprayed, so inquire before you assume. Next, become familiar with potentially dangerous and toxic inverts in your area (most centipedes are vicious and venomous; bees and

wasps are obviously bad food); avoid collecting and feeding these. Lastly, check with your state list of endangered species. Although few insects (mostly butterflies and beetles) are listed as endangered or threatened some are, and they are as deserving of conservation as bald eagles and San Francisco Garter

Cockroaches, large and small, are nutritious and readily taken foods for many lizards. Only cultured animals, like this startling *Blaberus giganteus,* must be fed to avoid the possibility of insecticide poisoning. Photo: R. Hunziker

Silkworm larvae rely on a diet of mulberry leaves for their nourishment, which made them difficult to maintain. The increasing availability of prepared food mixes has let them become more available to the average hobbyist. Photo: G. & C. Merker

immediately. Depending on the type of lizard in question, its age, and reproductive status, you should dust your feeder insects about every third feeding.

NOTES ON FEEDING INSECTS

When doing the actual feeding, there are several things to keep in mind. Most importantly, make sure the prey you are feeding is the appropriate size for the lizard. Lizards can injure themselves by eating insects that are too big for them. Also, if you feed the lizard overly large prey, it just may not eat—also not good. As a good rule of thumb, keep the size of the prey smaller than about half the size of the lizard's head, smaller for hatchlings. Prey of this size will not be a problem for lizards to consume.

Never feed more live insects to a lizard than it will eat within a few minutes. There are several reasons for this. One is that insects that escape the lizard and live in the cage lose much of their nutritional content. Also, any vitamin powder you conscientiously dusted onto the insects will soon be rubbed off

wheat bran, or crushed cereal. That is the base food. For water, give the crickets a piece of sweet potato, carrot, or orange that has been dusted with the vitamin/mineral powder. Keep your crickets in this setup for 12 to 24 hours before feeding them out. Mealworms can be gut-loaded similarly. If you are feeding your insects a nutritious diet normally and dusting them regularly, you will only need to gut-load your insects once every five or so feedings. This depends

somewhat on the lizard being fed; hatchlings and breeding females should receive gut-loaded prey about twice as often as normal.

Vitamin dusting is an easy way to provide necessary nutrients to your lizards. In simple terms, put the feeder insects into a plastic bag or a jar, add some powdered vitamin/mineral supplements, and gently shake or swish the container around. The insects become covered in the powder and are ready to be fed to your lizards

A good reptile-grade calcium (low phosphorus) and vitamin supplement powder makes it easier to increase the nutritional value of crickets and other foods. Photo: M. Walls

Carnivorous lizards and larger omnivores will take small mice as a major part of the diet or the occasional supplement. This eight-day-old fuzzy mouse is a good size for many monitors and larger blue-tongued skinks. Photo: M. Walls

Though cute and hard to think of as food, baby button quail (Turnix) are easy to find and make a good addition to the diet of many carnivorous lizards. Photo: M. Walls

earthworms), ground turkey, eggs, *cooked* chicken, small chicks and ducklings (available through several reptile food suppliers), and high-quality canned cat food. There are also several brands of canned monitor and tegu food on the market that provide excellent nutrition. For those species known to eat such fare in the wild, you can include fish and shellfish in the diet. Feeding a variety is more nutritious and certainly more interesting for the lizard.

Other than the invertebrates, prey should be pre-killed to avoid having a rodent severely bite or scratch your lizard as it fights for its life. Although many carnivorous lizards eat lizards, snakes, frogs, and other herps naturally, these are not recommended as food, as the chance of passing on parasites is relatively high. Captive-bred herps might be all right to feed to other lizards, but I think most herpers would have difficulty offering herps as food.

onto the substrate, hidebox, and other cage furniture. Escaped insects eventually get hungry, and when they get hungry, they get dangerous. Feeder insects, especially crickets and mealworms, have been known to attack lizards. This has resulted in lizards missing feet, eyes, and tail tips, and has even caused fatalities. Lastly, insects that have escaped your lizard may soon escape the cage. It's no fun to wake up in bed with a cricket crawling on your face.

CARNIVORES

Most of the larger lizards are carnivores. In nature, they prey primarily on other vertebrates, including mammals, birds, reptiles, amphibians, fish (in some cases), and eggs of birds and reptiles. What exactly the lizard preys upon is determined by many things including the species of lizard, the habitat, and the availability of the various types of prey. Most carnivorous lizards eat a variety of different vertebrates and also eat larger invertebrates.

Several carnivorous lizards eat a significant number of other lizards. It therefore seems illogical that feeding a carnivorous lizard "just mice" would be adequate. As with the insectivores, strive for variety in the diet. What this means is that, in addition to the easily come-by mice, you should feed the lizards large invertebrates (giant roaches, grasshoppers, large

It's a lizard-eat-lizard world out there, and small, inexpensive lizards such as Turkish Geckos, *Hemidactylus turcicus*, make a good treat for many carnivores. Photo: R. D. Bartlett

BREEDING TECHNIQUES

Many keepers aspire to be breeders, often with dreams of piles of cash to be made by captive-producing one lizard or another. Although breeding is fun and educational, it rarely is profitable. Sorry to shock you with reality, but this is the truth. Most of the easily bred lizards are now bred in such numbers that the cost of producing each individual is very close to the price one can get for it.

That aside, it must be said that captive-breeding is important for the hobby of lizard keeping. Wild populations are increasingly threatened and holding/shipping conditions often are inhumane. The answer to these problems is to captive-breed our lizards, to captive-breed lizards in such numbers that wild collection of specimens will be unnecessary save for providing fresh genetic material. Thus keepers are encouraged to captive-breed their lizards if they can definitely place the offspring in good homes, if the species in question is not frequently bred in captivity, or if the species in question is endangered or threatened in the wild. Also, in some areas of the country some species will be bred more frequently and be more available than others. Breeding one of the species that is scarce in your area will provide a welcome source of captive-bred offspring for the herpers in your region, rather than contributing to the local overpopulation of a given species.

This section is just a brief introduction to the breeding of lizards. More specific breeding information is given in the sections on the various species and groups of lizards.

SEXING

The first difficulty to surmount in the breeding of lizards is being sure you have a sexual pair. In many lizards,

Male lizards often are more colorful than females of the same species. A fine example of this is the swifts, such as *Sceloporus occidentalis*, where the males have large iridescent blue patches on the belly and throat.
Photo: M. Smith

determining the sex of a specimen is easy, in others nearly impossible, and most fall in between. It normally helps if you have many lizards of a given species to compare and that all those being sexed are adults. Hatchlings of most species are nearly impossible to sex. For some lizards, you may have to look at several indications of sex to be positive of the animal's gender.

Across many groups of lizards, the male is more colorful than the female. Additionally, if the species has crests, frills, dewlaps, or other ornamentation, the ornaments of the male will be larger and more developed. This is especially true in the families Agamidae, Iguanidae, Polychrotidae, and Chamaeleonidae. Males in most lizard species are the larger sex and often have

Large femoral pores, especially those obviously secreting a waxy substance, mark the males of many lizards. This is an earless lizard, *Cophosaurus texanus*, of the southwestern U.S. Photo: K. H. Switak

larger, bulkier heads.

In several families, the males develop enlarged pores on the undersides of the thighs. These are called femoral pores. In the species that have them, the females generally have the pores present but they are much smaller than those of the males. The pores of the males sometimes secrete a thick wax thought to be used as a territorial marking. The pores

The hemipenial bulge is obvious in this male New Caledonian Crested Gecko, *Rhacodactylus ciliatus*. When present, the bulge may be the surest way of telling males from females at a glance. Photo: R. D. Bartlett

are seen most often in the Iguanidae, Phynosomatidae, Cordylidae, Agamidae, Eublepharidae, and Gekkonidae.

Male lizards and snakes have paired copulatory organs called the hemipenes. (Technically, this is a single penis split to the base, but the two halves usually are thought of as independent organs.) At rest, these lie in pockets near the vent in the base of the tail. In many species, you can sex a lizard by looking for a swelling, usually paired, in the area just behind the vent. These are called the hemipenial bulges, as the swelling is caused by the presence of the hemipenes. Therefore, if you see hemipenial bulges, the individual is male. This method of sexing works particularly well with species in Chamaeleonidae, Gekkonidae, and Eublepharidae. When the male is about to mate, the hemipenes engorge with blood and fold outward. In many snakes, one can manually evert the hemipenes with some pressure applied just behind the vent. This works in some lizard species too, but as so many lizard shed their tails, great care must be taken. Additionally, too much pressure or a rough job may cause internal damage to the poor creature. Do not try to manually evert hemipenes until some experienced person shows you how to do it. Everting works on some members of Scincidae and Agamidae and probably other families as well. A variation on this technique is used to sex monitors, a group notoriously difficult to determine. A

syringe of warm saline is injected into the base of the tail, the pressure of the fluid causing the hemipenes to evert. Sometimes male lizards will evert their hemipenes when stressed or when defecating.

It should go without saying that if your lizard lays eggs it is absolutely a female.

If you really want to breed your lizards successfully, I recommend having at least five individuals, two males and three females. This protects you from infertility, unexpected deaths, and pair incompatibility. Also, in some species, male-male competition can help stimulate breeding.

BEFORE YOU BREED

Breeding is stressful to the animals involved. Therefore, you must take excellent care of your breeders year-round. They should be given the best diet and keeping conditions you can offer them. Never breed lizards that are in any but the best of health. Breeding weak or unhealthy individuals is completely unethical as it often leads to the death of the parents (especially the female) and frequently produces weak and unhealthy young. If your breeders appear to be at all ill or "not right," put off breeding them until they are back in perfect condition.

SETTING THE MOOD

Unfortunately, lizards, unlike mice and rats, don't always breed if you just put males and females together and take good care of them. The reason for this lies in their natural environment. In most habitats, some times of

the year have conditions that are more favorable for the survival of baby lizards. These are the times when the temperatures, humidity, food supply, and other factors are at their best for the survival of the offspring of that species. A lizard doesn't just know when this time is; it is told so by subtle cues in its surroundings. These cues act on various centers in the brain and on the reproductive and endocrine systems to stimulate the lizard to produce young at the proper times. The system has been fine-tuned by natural selection so that lizards don't waste their reproductive energies by laying eggs at a time when those eggs would surely never hatch.

Often it is not the conditions themselves that stimulate reproduction but the *change* in conditions that does so. This is the key to breeding lizards of many species. You must provide a change in the conditions in which you keep your lizards. This does not mean to change things randomly; certain factors in the environment are more important to change than others, and there is a range in which the changes should be made. In some cases, breeding is most successful if several different keeping conditions are changed rather than just one. All changes should be made gradually, usually over the course of about two weeks.

Light is one of the most important factors in the reproduction of lizards. In most areas of the world, the amount of daylight changes seasonally. Many lizards use this change in photoperiod as

a cue for reproduction. By varying the length of time you keep your lizards' lights on, you may be able to stimulate them to breed. For most lizards, keeping them with 12 hours of light and 12 hours of dark is the normal condition; for ones that are strongly diurnal (day-active), many keepers use a photoperiod of 14:10, light:dark. When you want to breed lizards, you should gradually cut back on the photoperiod. During the dark "winter," you'll want the opposite photoperiod, 10:14. Maintain this reduced photoperiod for at least two months, then gradually return it to normal. Once the lights have been returned to normal levels, the lizards should be ready to breed in a few weeks. Having your lights on timers greatly eases this process.

In nature, when daylength gets shorter, the temperatures start to get cooler. Temperature is another parameter that can be manipulated to breed lizards. The normal keeping temperatures can be thought of as the summer. You will want to provide a winter and then another summer. To do this, gradually drop your keeping temperature to a winter low. You can do this by setting your thermostat lower, changing the wattage of bulbs you are using, etc. How much you drop the temperature will depend greatly on the species you are keeping. For most lizards a five- or ten-degree drop is adequate. During this cooling period, the lizards may eat very little or not at all and become very inactive. This is normal. After at least two months, return temperatures slowly to

normal. Feed them very heavily once they become interested in food again. Most lizards mate after the temperatures warm up, but some will mate during the cooling period. Do some research on the species you plan on breeding so you know during what season it normally mates. If it mates in the cool period, you will need to have your pairs together while they are cooling.

Temperature and photoperiod are the two most important factors to vary when breeding lizards. They can easily be varied together. When the photoperiod is at its shortest, temperatures should be at their lowest. This is what the lizards would experience in the wild. Cycling the temperature and light together is much more likely to give you baby lizards than cycling either one by itself.

In some species, especially those that come from equatorial rain forests, there is little variation in seasonal photoperiod or temperature. However, there are pronounced rainy and dry seasons. Thus, the humidity is the primary cue that they use to determine when to reproduce. For these species, you will want to vary the level of relative humidity in your cage seasonally. Give the lizards a dry period with the humidity at the low end of their range of tolerance and slightly lower temperatures for two months followed by a rise in the humidity and plenty of misting. Humidity is not frequently given as much consideration as temperature and photoperiod, and its importance for many species is not understood. Similarly,

there has been little research as to what other factors play roles in the stimulation of reptile reproduction. Such things as availability of specific types of food, abundance of food, frequency of storms, and population size play some as yet unknown role in lizard reproduction.

IT DIDN'T WORK

If cycling temperature and photoperiod did not stimulate mating in your lizards, there are several things to think about. The first may be that your lizards aren't old enough to breed yet. Most larger lizards mature at around two years of age; many smaller lizards are mature in under a year. However, this varies by species, individual, and keeping conditions. You can wait and cycle them again next year.

If you have been housing your pairs together all year long, try separating the males from the females and cycling again. When you return them to summer conditions, reintroduce the sexes. This often does the trick.

You could try to shuffle your pairs. While some would say lizards don't have personal likes and dislikes, sometimes a given pair of lizards will just not breed with each other, while the same female may be very receptive to a different male in your collection. Pair the individuals differently and see if this helps.

In those species that are territorial, it may help to introduce another male into the group. This may start some territorial squabbling between the males, which often leads to mating. If you

This clutch of Green Iguana eggs is being incubated in a homemade styrofoam box incubator. Though such simple incubators lack the features of more expensive commercial equipment, they work well enough to be used by many breeders. Photo: J. Prime

per week would be great. Avoid handling her, and reduce her stress level as much as possible.

When it comes time for her to lay eggs, she must have a suitable nesting site. This usually consists of a sheltered area with a damp substrate in which she can dig a nest. A food storage container with a hole cut in it works for small lizards; larger ones can be given a nesting box made from plastic shoeboxes, cat litter pans, or garbage cans. The normal substrates are vermiculite, sand, sphagnum moss, and potting soil, varying with species and the choice of the keeper. However, there are many variations. Provide your female with the proper type of nest for her species. Most species of live-bearing lizards do not need a nesting box, but they may give birth in their hidebox or in some other sheltered area. The failure to

do this, you must watch the group carefully. Males of some species can become vicious toward each other. If the combat is fierce, remove the male that seems to be losing (you can shift a female into his cage right away and see if he'll mate despite his bruised ego) and let the winner breed the females.

eating, it is beneficial to give her some extra calcium in her food and extra vitamins as well. Don't overdo it, but an extra serving of vitamins once

An easily purchased electronic thermometer with probe is the best way to monitor incubation temperatures and humidity. The sex of some lizards depends on their incubation temperature, so this must be kept accurate within one to three degrees. Photo: *Pogona vitticeps* eggs, M. Walls

THE MOTHER TO BE

Once your lizards have bred, you will want to give the female some extra consideration to make sure she is able to produce the greatest number of the healthiest young possible. Most of the time, it is best to separate her into her own enclosure that provides her with optimal keeping conditions. You should feed her heavily, realizing she may stop eating completely for several weeks before parturition. While she is still

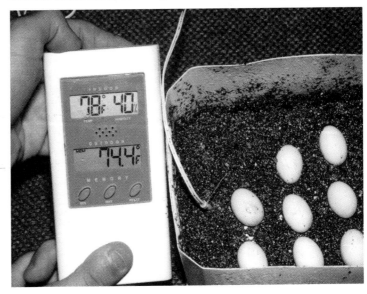

Deli cups make good incubator egg containers for small lizards. These hatchling Texas Banded Geckos, *Coleonyx brevis*, are shedding before their first meal. Photo: G. & C. Merker

and plug it in. Place the lid on the box and measure the temperature in 12 hours or so. If it is too low or high, adjust accordingly and monitor closely for 48 hours before placing the eggs inside. A food storage container half-filled with *just moist* vermiculite or sand generally serves as the egg container. When transferring the eggs from the nesting box to the egg container, move them without turning or jarring them; such roughness may kill the embryos. Once they are in the container, place it on top of the bricks inside the incubator. Keep an eye on the temperature and water levels during incubation. Do not disturb the eggs except to check them occasionally. Remove any obviously bad eggs unless they are glued to good ones; pulling bad eggs off of good eggs can kill the good eggs. When the time comes for the eggs to hatch, check them daily. Hatchlings should be removed to correctly set-up cages after they completely emerge from the egg.

provide your lizard with a proper nest will often cause her to retain her eggs, a condition called egg-binding. This is fatal if not given immediate veterinary attention. If she lays her eggs and there is no nest, she may scatter them about the cage or lay them in the water bowl. In either case, the eggs usually die.

Once the female lays eggs, make sure she has access to plenty of food and water to replenish her resources.

INCUBATION

The eggs of most lizards will have to be incubated by the keeper. Left in the nesting box in the cage, they usually do not hatch. An incubator provides the ideal conditions for hatching of the eggs. One can be bought or made, but in either case, it must be holding the proper conditions before you actually have eggs. Plan ahead.

A simple incubator to make at home requires a styrofoam fish shipping box, two bricks,

a 25-watt submersible aquarium heater, a thermometer (preferably a digital one with external probe and ability to record minimum/maximum temperatures), water, and a container for the eggs. Place the bricks in the bottom of the styrofoam box and fill with water until the level is just below the top of the bricks. Put the heater in the water

Culling of deformed hatchlings is essential when trying to breed the best specimens. This earless lizard, *Holbrookia lacerata*, has a grossly deformed head and probably would never live long. Photo: P. Freed

THE GREEN DRAGONS: IGUANAS, WATER DRAGONS, BASILISKS, AND ANOLES

The most popular pet reptile today is the Giant Green Iguana (*Iguana iguana*). Baby iguanas have cute, Kermit the Frog faces and a beautiful emerald color. Adults are sizable creatures with a stunning appearance and often become quite tame. A few other lizards require similar care to the Green Iguana and are not very dissimilar in size or appearance. These include the swift-footed basilisks (*Basiliscus* spp.) of Central and South America and the semi-aquatic Green Water Dragons (*Physignathus cocincinus*) of Southeast Asia. Since many aspects of the biology of these animals are so similar, they can be treated together. Also, for convenience I've included here a few lines about the anoles (*Anolis*), which often remind beginners of tiny iguanas and are not that dissimilar in their requirements.

Young Giant Green Iguanas, *Iguana iguana*, lack the large dewlaps and high crests of adults, but they tend to have the brightest green colors. Photo: I. Francais

Notice the conical scales on the neck of this half-grown *Iguana iguana*—and also the scarring on the snout from when the animal has run into the walls of its cage. Photo: I. Francais

Antillean Iguanas, *Iguana delicatissima*, lack the round scale behind the jaws found in the more common species. This iguana is seldom seen, protected in its native islands, and virtually unavailable. Photo: Marian Bacon

GREEN IGUANAS

Out of this grouping of saurians, the Giant Green Iguana is perhaps the most common, most familiar, and largest. Adult males of this species can reach 6 feet in length or more; females often reach 5 feet. They are heavy-bodied animals with long, slender tails. They bear a crest of flexible but spiky looking scales down the back and an erectile banner of flesh beneath the throat (called a dewlap). These two structures are more developed in males than in females and are barely apparent in hatchlings. On the nape, iguanas have several rows of conical scales, some having a sharp point. Below the corner of the jaw is a large, flat, shiny scale. This character sets the Green Iguana apart from the Antillean Iguana (*I. delicatissima*), a nearly identical species that lacks the large scale. There is a small whitish scale on top of the head, equidistant between the tops of the eyes, that covers the parietal eye, which can sense light and helps an iguana to determine when it has been in the sun for too long. Many other diurnal lizards also have a parietal eye, including the other lizards discussed in this chapter.

The tail makes up about two-thirds of the total length, becoming more slender and whip-like distally (toward the tip). The tail is an iguana's primary defense; one or two smacks from it and most predators will find an easier meal. The feet have elongated toes, each ending in a sharp claw. The fourth toe on each hind foot is especially elongated. In adult males, femoral pores are large and secrete a thick, waxy substance used as a territorial marking.

Given that the most common name for this animal is the Giant Green Iguana, it is no surprise that the coloration is primarily green. There is much variation, and some iguanas may be browner, grayer, or bluer than others. The young are a much brighter green than the adults, and males are usually brighter than females. There may be brown bands on the trunk, and most iguanas have brown banding on the tail. Males often develop extensive orange coloration on the forequarters when in breeding condition.

GREEN WATER DRAGONS

Green Water Dragons appear very similar to iguanas, but they do not reach such a tremendous size.

Breeding adult Chinese Water Dragons often develop a bright pink glow to the lips and chin. Photo: K. H. Switak

Chinese Water Dragons, *Physignathus cocincinus*, are in many ways better pets than Giant Green Iguanas—they are a bit smaller, tamer, easier to feed, and bred in captivity on a more regular basis. Adults often stay bright green.
Photo: Marian Bacon

The common striped basilisk of the terrarium hobby is _Basiliscus vittatus_, the Northern Brown Basilisk. Photo: J. Gerholdt

At most a Water Dragon will reach 4 feet, two-thirds of this being tail. Water Dragons also use their tail as a weapon. In general, Water Dragons are not as heavy-bodied as iguanas, but as in iguanas, males are larger than females. On the nape there is a relatively high crest, much more developed in the male. This crest may be flushed with blue or yellow in large, reproductively active animals, and a rosy cast may occur on the lips and chin in breeders. Adult Water Dragons often retain the vibrant greens of the young. The body often has transverse brown bands that may fade with age; the tail is similarly banded and may be mostly brown.

BASILISKS

The basilisks are a group of four species of good-sized, semi-aquatic, semi-arboreal lizards. Three species appear in the hobby with some regularity; the fourth, the Red-headed Basilisk (_B. galeritus_), the only species in the group that has no cresting on the back, only rarely appears in the pet trade. Two species are brown and difficult to tell apart: the Double-crested Basilisk (_B. basiliscus_) and the Northern Brown Basilisk (_B. vittatus_). The best way to tell one of these from the other is to look at the scales of the belly: in the Northern Brown they will be keeled and in the Double-crested they will be smooth. When fully adult, the Double-crested has a much higher crest than the other. Most of the animals in the hobby are Northern Browns, rather than Double-cresteds. The most spectacular species is the Green Basilisk (_B. plumifrons_). This animal is bright green

with black and white markings. Males bear splendid crests on the head, back, and tail. Not only is this the most attractive species in the genus, but it is also the one most often captive-bred. Oddly, these animals often turn pale blue in captivity.

Basilisks are smaller than iguanas or Green Water Dragons. Green Basilisks reach a length of 30 inches, and the other three species usually do not exceed 2 feet in length. In all species the male may be up to 6 inches longer than the female. The tail is up to three-quarters of the total length.

In their countries of origin, basilisks often are referred to as "Jesus Christ lizards." This comes from their astounding ability to run across the surface of ponds and rivers. They can do this not only because of their great speed, but because of structural adaptations of the feet. They also are given to running bipedally when pursued. These are swift and active lizards often injured by collisions with their cages.

ANOLES

Though they are much smaller than iguanas and the other lizards in this chapter, to many hobbyists the anoles, genus _Anolis_, are just like tiny iguanas. Often misleadingly called American chameleons until just a few years ago, the Green Anole, _Anolis carolinensis_, and the Brown Anole, _Anolis sagrei_, are to be found in virtually every pet shop and, because of their low price, often are sold to absolute beginners. These are not the best of pets for a beginner, however, as they are

Few lizards can match the glory of a captive-bred male Green Basilisk, *Basiliscus plumifrons*, in good health. Unfortunately, many specimens turn bluish in the terrarium and suffer from infections of the crests.
Photo: Marian Bacon

somewhat fragile lizards that require a varied diet of insects and relatively humid, well-ventilated terrariums. They are great escape artists, the widened pads on their feet allowing them to run up glass surfaces and out the cage any time the terrarium is opened for maintenance. Like other tropical and subtropical lizards, they require basking lamps during the day and should be kept over 72F all year (about 88F near the basking lights). Males are exceedingly territorial, defending their spots by flaring a brightly colored fold (dewlap) under the throat and grappling with intruders. Females of some anoles, though they lack the dewlap, may be as aggressive as males. Most species are some 6 to 8 inches in length and vary from bright green to subdued browns and grays;

most can change color rapidly with mood. In addition to the two abundant small species usually sold, the much larger (to nearly 20 inches) Knight Anole, *Anolis equestris,* sometimes is available. This species will take young mice and also likes ripe fruit as diet supplements. Most anoles lay two hard-shelled eggs in soil at the base of plants in the male's territory.

HOUSING

Iguanas, basilisks, and Green Water Dragons live in tropical forests, and all are most frequently found near water. They all climb and swim very well and are swift runners. This translates into needing large, humid, warm enclosures in captivity.

Most keepers will start with glass aquariums for these lizards, and this type of housing works well until the

animal becomes too big for an aquarium. For a hatchling of any of these species, use at least a 20-gallon long aquarium; a 30-gallon would be preferable. Get a sturdy screen top for it, preferably one that can hold the weight of heat lamps. For adults, much larger cages will be needed. All of these animals like to climb, so give them some height. Iguanas will use all the space you can provide. A cage measuring 6 feet long by 2 or 3 feet wide by 4 feet high is the minimum I'd recommend for a full-grown animal. Add about 50% to each measurement if keeping a pair or trio. Adult Green Water Dragons and basilisks should be given at least 4 feet of length, 2 feet of width, and 2 feet of height. In all cases, larger cages would be advisable. When keeping a group of adult iguanas, giving

Though few advanced hobbyists keep them and they are far from good pets, Green Anoles, *Anolis carolinensis*, are among the first lizards bought by many fanciers. Photo: R. D. Bartlett

Knight Anoles, *Anolis equestris*, are large, colorful anoles, but unfortunately most specimens seen in the shops are dehydrated, scarred, and cold. Photo: I. Francais

them a small room would not be unreasonable.

For the bottom of the cage, many different substrates have been used by different keepers; each keeper has their own preference. I do not recommend cedar shavings (they're toxic to reptiles), other wood shavings (they get very moldy and unpleasant in the humidity these lizards require), rabbit pellets, sand, or gravel. Newspaper and paper towels can be used and are absorbent, inexpensive, and harmless to your pet. However, they must be changed daily, which quickly becomes a chore. The reptile barks sold in many pet stores are excellent. Potting soil is an option, but it tends to be messy. If you opt to use it, buy a brand that has no perlite or styrofoam in it; these materials may be ingested by a lizard and cause intestinal blockages. Recycled paper bedding may be used, but it might fungus quickly in the warm and humid

conditions. Whatever bedding you use, be sure to remove feces daily and to change the entire substrate as needed.

All of these lizards bask on sunny limbs, rocks, and river banks to warm themselves to acceptable levels. Heat lamps are the best way to keep these lizards properly warm. Undertank heaters can be used for supplemental heat, but these lizards may not spend much time on the bottom of the cage (especially iguanas), making the devices almost useless. During the day the warm end of the cage should be in the middle to upper 80s and the cool end 79 to 82F. A basking limb should reach up near the heat light, providing a basking spot that reaches a temperature of 95 to 105F. (Be sure the light is adequately screened so a lizard cannot burn itself.) If housing your lizards in pairs or groups, you may need to have a basking spot for each individual. Watch them closely to be sure that none

are excluded from the hot spot by more aggressive individuals. At night, the temperature of the cage can drop safely to 75F. Never should the cage become colder than 70F, especially for the basilisks. In addition to heat lamps, these lizards must be given full-spectrum lighting to provide vitamin D.

To provide proper humidity, a sizable water vessel and a plant mister should be used. These animals should be sprayed lightly once a day. The basilisks and Water Dragons may need an additional spraying in the evening if the cage dries out too much. Water Dragons should have a water bowl big enough for them to get their whole body into; this is also good for the other two. The water bowl probably will need daily cleaning. Give them sturdy climbing materials. The basilisks, being nervous and flighty lizards, should be housed with plenty of cover. Otherwise, they will be anxious, running into the glass constantly. Plastic, silk, and live plants make good cover, as do branches, rocks, and sturdy hideboxes. Cover usually is not important for Water Dragons and iguanas, but it will be if you happen to purchase a particularly nervous individual.

DIFFERENT DIETS

In terms of keeping these magnificent dragons, the biggest difference between them is the diet. Iguanas are nearly total herbivores, basilisks are mostly insectivores/carnivores, and Water Dragons are omnivores.

When they are juveniles, basilisks and Water Dragons

can be fed on a staple diet of crickets, mealworms, waxworms, and other insects. These active lizards should be fed daily; hatchlings probably should receive food twice a day for their first six months of life. Feed your insects a good diet before feeding them to your lizards. For hatchlings, one meal each day should be dusted with vitamin/mineral powder. When the lizards are older and receiving only one meal daily, dust the insects roughly twice a week. Adults may also be fed larger insects, such as roaches and June beetles, and small mice. Vary the diet of your lizards and that of the feeder insects as well. Some individuals will take live fish, dried krill, live crayfish, and other similar foods. Experiment.

Iguanas feed largely on leaves in the wild, and you must strive to duplicate this diet in captivity. The vast majority of an iguana's diet should be leafy green vegetables. The best ones to feed are collards, mulberry leaves, mustard greens, turnip greens, dandelion leaves, escarole, endive, and parsley. Avoid iceberg lettuce, which is mostly water and low in nutrients. Spinach, chard, and beet greens have high concentrations of oxalic acid, which binds with calcium making it unavailable for absorption into the body. Cabbage, broccoli, kale, and related vegetables contain a chemical that interferes with the production and function of the thyroid hormones. Therefore, these leafy vegetables should only be offered in moderation. Although most of the diet

should be composed of leafy greens, other vegetables and some fruits should be included also. Keep the percentage of fruits down to the level of an occasional treat, since most fruits are high in sugars but low in calcium and other minerals. Papayas and raspberries are exceptions, being very rich in calcium. Some good vegetables to include are bell peppers, squash, carrots (grated or shredded, including the leaves), corn, okra, sweet potatoes (grated or shredded), green beans, peas (include pods and leaves), and asparagus. Feed iguanas daily with the various vegetables shredded or chopped into bite-sized pieces. Make sure you are feeding them enough; iguanas tend to eat a lot of food. Twice weekly into adulthood, add a tiny amount of vitamin/mineral powder to the food. Some keepers continue this practice with adults, but others believe this is harmful since the adults

have lower nutrient requirements. If you are attempting breeding, be sure to give extra food, calcium, and vitamins to the females.

Water Dragons often will eat significant amounts of plant matter if it is offered. They tend to be more partial to fruit than to vegetables. It would be beneficial to provide them with a weekly salad of mixed fruits and vegetables.

In most cases, these three lizards are easier to acquire as wild-caught (or farm-raised in the case of iguanas) imports. Only the Green Basilisk is bred with any frequency. If you can find captive-bred examples of these magnificent dragons, purchase them rather than imports, even though you undoubtedly will pay more for them.

BREEDING

If you have the room and interest, you should try to breed your basilisks, iguanas, and/or Water Dragons. You will not get rich by doing so,

Prepared commercial iguana foods can offer a fortified diet including such items as real flower blossoms and berries. Photo courtesy of Kaytee Products, Inc.

but you will learn a lot and be able to provide some captive-bred offspring to individuals who may otherwise have to purchase wild-caught animals.

These lizards normally will breed when given a seasonal cycle of temperatures and photoperiod. Cycling the humidity may also be helpful. Iguanas are the most difficult to breed of this group. They breed best when kept outdoors at least part of the year. Temperatures should gradually be reduced until they are roughly five and no more than ten degrees cooler than the normal keeping temperatures. Keep them in these conditions for about eight weeks and then gradually return them to normal.

The lizards should show interest in mating a few weeks after the return to normal conditions. In iguanas, mating sometimes occurs near the end of the cooling period.

After several matings, it is best to separate the females. In the Water Dragons, basilisks, and iguanas, a container of moistened sand or vermiculite will serve as a nesting site. Provide a container properly sized for the lizard in question. Iguanas will need kitchen garbage pails or other suitably large containers for their nests. The other lizards should be happy with larger cat litter pans. The eggs can be incubated on vermiculite with high humidity. A temperature of 80 to 90F works for the basilisks. Iguana eggs should not be incubated at temperatures below 84F. Basilisks lay one or two (sometimes as many as four) clutches of 15 to 25 eggs per breeding season. Water Dragons lay up to five clutches of roughly 15 eggs. Rarely do iguanas lay more than one clutch in a season, but their clutches are large, typically 35 to 50 eggs with an extreme of 80. Water Dragon and basilisk eggs take roughly 60 to 80 days to hatch. Iguanas take somewhat longer, in the range of 75 to 120 days. The hatchlings should be kept in an optimum environment and not exposed to extremes of temperature. It is best to keep them very humid for the first several days. Hatchlings of all of these lizards should start eating within four days of hatching and are likely to eat sooner. Raising them separately or in small groups will allow you to keep track of their condition better than if kept in larger groups.

Breeding any of the green dragons is not common in the terrarium, but all are worth a try. This pair of turquoise Chinese Green Water Dragons is preparing to mate. Photo: S. McKeown

CHAMELEONS: LIONS IN THE TREES

One of the families of lizards that attract herpers and nonherpers alike is the chameleons. Many people are taken with their attractive colors, sloth-slow movements, and bizarre structure. In some ways, chameleons appear more extraterrestrial than saurian. Although these animals are interesting and desirable to keepers, they are not for everyone. They have exacting requirements not easily met by most keepers. Most species are delicate, quickly succumbing to inadequate husbandry. Wild-caught chameleons normally are stressed, dehydrated, and loaded with parasites. Veterinary care usually is required to establish these individuals.

However, a small number of chameleon species are now being captive-bred and can be recommended to keepers who have some experience with other lizards. It is this handful of species that we will be discussing. First, a guide to general chameleon care.

Chameleons are members of the family Chamaeleonidae. The family can be found in Africa, Madagascar, several other islands in the Indian Ocean, the Middle East, southern Europe, and India. The greatest number of species is found on Madagascar and in sub-Saharan Africa. Most chameleons are flattened laterally, their bodies more or less resembling leaves in

shape. They have small eyes mounted on turrets. Their eyes are highly mobile, and each one can move independently of the other, allowing a chameleon to keep watch in several directions simultaneously. They are slow and wary, yet are efficient predators.

One of the most spectacular adaptations to being slow, arboreal insectivores is their long, sticky tongue. A chameleon's tongue is generally at least as long as its entire body. The end is sticky and somewhat flexible. A chameleon spying an insect takes careful aim and fires its tongue at the hapless bug. When the tongue hits, it folds around the insect to some degree, the sticky mucus also helping to hold it. The chameleon then reels in the morsel.

HOUSING

All of the chameleons commonly seen in the hobby are arboreal animals that are loathe to leave the trees. The word "chameleon" derives from the Greek, meaning "lion on the ground." However, most chameleons are at home only when high above the ground in the branches of trees. A better name would be "lion in the tree."

As tree-dwellers, chameleons do best when housed in tall cages—the taller the better. Most chameleons require good air flow. You will have more

success with this group of lizards if you house them in screened enclosures of some type. There are now several good cages on the market designed with chameleons in mind. Constructing a cage is also possible. The wire of the cage should not be abrasive to the lizard's feet. Rubberized wire is your best bet, but if you use it you must be careful that any heat lamps will not melt the rubber.

As a general rule, the common chameleons in the hobby can be broken into two groups: the tropical lowland animals and the humid mountain animals. There are differences in keeping these groups, especially as pertains to temperature. The lowland animals tend to be sun-worshipping lovers of warmth. They do best when they have a hot spot in the cage that reaches into the low 90s F; some species enjoy temperatures up to 100F for brief periods. The cool end of the cage should be in the upper 70s. The nighttime drop in temperature can be rather substantial, down to the mid-60s. The mountain species come from much cooler habitats. Although they are still technically tropical animals, they occur at high elevations that do not get nearly as warm as the lowlands. These animals do not do well if the temperatures get much higher than 83F. House montane chameleons with a weak

Few lizards can match a Panther Chameleon, *Chamaeleo pardalis*, in color. Unfortunately, only a few species of chameleons are keepable by any but patient, knowledgeable hobbyists. Photo: Marian Bacon

basking light, the temperature beneath which should not be higher than 82 to 85F. The rest of the enclosure can be completely unheated. At the coolest point, the temperature can safely be as low as 65F. At night, a drop of at least 10 degrees is preferred. Most montane chameleons can survive temperatures in the low 40s or lower, so heating them at night is not normally a concern. All chameleons should be given full-spectrum lighting.

Both types of chameleons need to be kept in relatively humid conditions. Mist them several times a day. Keeping them with live plants will help keep the cage humid and provide additional climbing surfaces. Ficus trees, pothos ivy, and hibiscus plants are great plants to include. The montane species seem to have more strict humidity requirements than the others. These should be kept rather wet, given the opportunity to dry when they desire. If you keep chameleons, having rain-makers, fog machines, and/or automatic misters will great facilitate your keeping chores. Aside from humidity, many chameleons will only drink water that is moving. When you mist them, make sure that most surfaces of the cage are dripping. Additionally, you will do well to provide a water dripper. These can be purchased or made by taking a plastic container, poking one or two tiny holes in the bottom, and partially filling it with water. Place it on top of the cage, allowing it to drip through plants and climbing branches into a bowl. I can not over-emphasize the importance of proper hydration in the successful keeping of chameleons.

Along with some plants, chameleons must have climbing materials. These should vary in diameter to provide the chameleon's feet with proper exercise. Some options include natural branches (cleaned and sterilized, of course), wooden dowels, fake branches, and artificial vines (wonderful products). Although most chameleons like to have substantial cover, they also like to have branch "highways" to travel upon through the cage.

With some notable exceptions, chameleons are antisocial animals. They should be housed singly,

Almost all available chameleons do best in tall, airy cages with many climbing branches and vines. Larger species, such as *Chamaeleo oustaleti*, may require small trees in an outdoor setting for best result. Photo: I. Francais

Most chameleons are very territorial, increasing the difficulties of housing them together. This pair of young (three months) Veiled Chameleons, *Chamaeleo calyptratus* (male with higher casque), is occupying the same cage—and vine. Most chameleons can be kept as trios if the owner is careful and gives the lizards lots of cover. Photo: P. Freed

unless you have enclosures approaching the size of a small room. In some cases, notably with Veiled Chameleons, the animals should not even be within visual range of each other, as they will spend all of their time stressed-out, trying to defend their territories from the perceived invader. Breeding attempts are made by housing the male and female in adjacent cages for a day or two and then introducing the female to the male. Montane species seem to more social than the lowland ones and can be kept in groups of one male and two to four females.

FEEDING

Wild-caught adult chameleons can be stubborn feeders. With these animals, cockroaches, king mealworms, or caterpillars often stimulate feeding. Variety is extremely important in the chameleon diet. Chameleons have been known to stop eating when they have been fed a monotonous diet of crickets or mealworms. Crickets make a good staple, but rotate in as many different feeder bugs as you can get your hands on. Don't forget to feed the insects a nutritious diet and to vitamin dust them two or three times weekly. Most chameleons eat large quantities of insects. Feed them daily or twice a day.

BREEDING

Breeding chameleons, with the exception of a handful of species, is rather rare. Most will breed if they are kept in excellent conditions, exposed to natural sunlight, and given some mild cycling of the photoperiod. Several species give birth to live young, meaning there is no need for a nest box or an incubator. The ones that lay eggs tend to dig rather deep nests. Fill a small garbage can to a depth at least equal to the length of the chameleon in question. Put a branch in the can for her to climb on and a basking light above. She should dig down to the bottom and lay her eggs. Remove them carefully to an incubator. Most chameleon eggs incubate very nicely at room temperature. Perlite is the usual incubation media rather than vermiculite, especially for Veiled Chameleons, the most commonly bred form. The eggs take a long time to hatch, from six months in some species to over a year in Parson's

Chameleon and a few others. Baby chameleons are minuscule and need tiny fruitflies and pinhead crickets for food. They grow rapidly and need a highly nutritious diet.

SOME SPECIES

The most commonly seen chameleon in today's hobby is the Veiled Chameleon, *Chamaeleo calyptratus*. This is the hardiest species and really the only one that is even somewhat keepable by a herp novice (a novice is still much better off starting with a Leopard Gecko, Bearded Dragon, or blue-tongued skink). Veileds are also one of the most colorful of chameleons, especially the males, which are green with yellow, blue, and red-brown markings. They also have extremely tall casques, the bony crests on the head. The males reach a length of 18 inches, females being no longer than a foot. The females have a much smaller casque and are not as brilliantly colored but still are very attractive. These chameleons come from desert canyons in Saudi Arabia and Yemen. They enjoy high temperatures in the day (up to 100F) and cool temperatures at night. They are more tolerant of low humidity than most chameleons, but they still do best in humid conditions. Adult Veileds will eat great amounts of vegetation and should be allowed to do so. Some sources believe roughly 50% of a Veiled Chameleon's diet should be leafy greens and flowers. Veileds are known for their large clutches of eggs; females have been know to produce over 70 eggs, the average being around 30.

Another commonly seen, though more expensive, chameleon is the Panther Chameleon, *C. pardalis*. These Madagascan chameleons are brilliantly colored and very variable. There are several color varieties, some restricted

Breeding chameleons allows the owner to observe a variety of color patterns in each sex based on age, condition, and mood. Females especially may have different patterns for each stage of their reproductive cycle. Juveniles seldom are as colorful as this young Panther Chameleon, *Chamaeleo pardalis*, from Ambanja, Madagascar. Photo: Marian Bacon

The large size, very high casque, and brilliant yellow and green colors mark the male Veiled Chameleon, *Chamaeleo calyptratus*. This fortunately also is one of the hardiest chameleons, tolerating both low and moderate humidity as well as a good span of temperatures. Photo: R. D. Bartlett

Young and female Veiled Chameleons lack the exaggerated casque of the male as well as the three broad yellow vertical bars on the side. The horizontal white bar over the shoulder usually indicates a female, but not always. Photo: A. Both

to a certain locality on their home island. Some are sea green, others dark red, still others are solid powder blue or banded in red, orange, and green; most varieties have at least the hint of a white stripe running down their sides. Males will reach up to 22 inches and females top out at 13. Keep this species as a lowland chameleon. Captive-bred babies are reasonably hardy, perhaps as hardy as Veileds. Panthers lay 20 to 50 eggs that hatch in 8 to 12 months. Incubate them at temperatures in the low 70s.

Oustalet's Chameleon, *C. oustaleti*, of Madagascar, is probably the largest of all the chameleons, with some males nearing 30 inches in length. Females are little more than half that size. House this species in appropriately sized cages outfitted for lowland species. They should have a basking spot that reaches 100F. In large enclosures, trios of one male and two females can be kept, provided there is plenty of cover, space, and food. Captive-bred offspring are among the hardiest of chameleons, though wild-caughts can be difficult to acclimate. Eggs incubate at room temperature or slightly warmer.

Last on the list of chameleons a beginner can consider is the Jackson's Chameleon, *C. jacksoni.* This African mountain species became common in the hobby after it was introduced and thrived on the Hawaiian

Islands. Keep them cool and very humid; they begin to suffer heat stress at temperatures around 85F. The males and females are nearly the same size, reaching lengths of up to a foot, though most are a few inches shorter. The males of the common subspecies in the hobby bear three horns on their head, one above each eye and one on the nose, but females lack horns or have at most small nubbins. These chameleons do well in small groups when given adequate space; do not house males together. Jackson's Chameleon frequently breeds in captivity. When you have a female that is pregnant, give her a slightly warmer

basking site than normal; one that reaches 85F would be adequate. These chameleons give live birth to up to 50 babies, though 20 is a more average number.

While there are many other species of chameleons available, these four are the only ones that should be considered by the beginner. The captive-bred offspring of some other species are not too difficult to keep, but most other species are only infrequently bred. If you wish to keep chameleons, first please read several of the books and magazine articles that are available on them. They are specialized, delicate, magnificent animals that require an informed and conscientious keeper.

Panther Chameleons, *Chamaeleo pardalis*, are famous for their brilliant colors that vary individually and with locality. Bright powder blue specimens, which come from just a few localities, are highly prized. Photo: S. McKeown

Oustalet's Chameleon, *Chamaeleo oustaleti*, is not especially colorful, and this green female is about as bright as the species gets. However, it is a hardy chameleon of impressive size and has a great future in the hobby. Photo: M. Burger

The three-horned Jackson's Chameleon, *Chamaeleo jacksoni*, may be the most familiar chameleon because it has been imported for decades. However, this live-bearer suffers from stress at higher temperatures and low humidity, making it difficult to maintain in many environments. Most specimens recently have come from Hawaii (where it was introduced), but that source may now have been eliminated. Photo: A. Both

GECKOS, GECKOS, EVERYWHERE

If you like lizards, you have certainly heard of geckos. These members of the families Gekkonidae and Eublepharidae are popular terrarium animals and are found throughout the tropics and subtropics worldwide. Gekkonidae is one of the largest families of the lizards, containing nearly 1,000 species. Some of the most popular geckos in the hobby today are the Leopard Gecko (*Eublepharis macularius*), Tokay Gecko (*Gekko gecko*), the flying geckos (*Ptychozoon* spp.), the day geckos (*Phelsuma* spp.), and the New Caledonian Crested Gecko (*Rhacodactylus ciliatus*).

COMMONALTIES

In a family as large and wide-ranging as Gekkonidae, the true geckos, there are tremendous differences in structure and habits. However, there are some things that all or most true geckos share in common. Perhaps the most readily apparent feature shared by true geckos is the lack of eyelids; the gecko-like lizards that have eyelids are members of a separate family, Eublepharidae, which includes the Leopard Gecko and is discussed later. In Gekkonidae the two eyelids have fused into a transparent scale, called a brille, covering the eye. This is one feature geckos share with snakes, although the groups do not appear to be closely related. To compensate for the inability to blink, geckos can clean their eyes with their tongues. Most geckos are nocturnal, although the day geckos are completely diurnal. Although there are quite a few terrestrial geckos, the majority are strong climbers bearing enlarged climbing pads on the toes. They have large eyes with vertical, often intricately scalloped pupils, a fine adaptation to seeing in low light conditions. With but a few exceptions, geckos have tiny, granular scales, often with scattered tuberculate scales on various parts of the body.

A molting *Rhacodactylus ciliatus* helps clean an eye with its tongue. Licking the eye, which lacks movable eyelids in the family Gekkonidae, is a very characteristic behavior of geckos in general and of few other lizards.
Photo: R. D. Bartlett

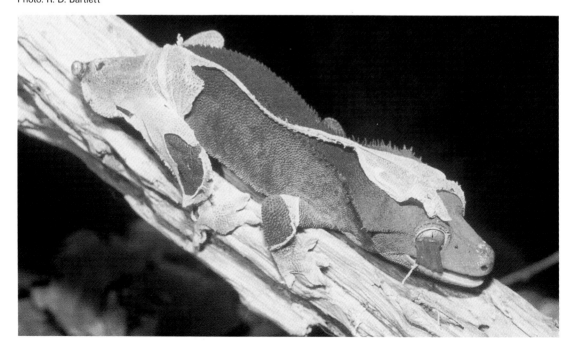

The large size and sometimes brilliant colors have made *Gekko gecko*, the Tokay Gecko, a popular terrarium pet, but this lizard actually has many problems associated with keeping it. It may be more difficult to handle than a beginner would assume. Photo: Dr. Z. Takacs

All geckos are primarily carnivorous. They eat whatever prey they can over-power and consume. In most cases, this means insects and other invertebrates primarily, but some geckos are large enough to eat other lizards, small birds, and small mammals. There are some geckos that eat a lot of vegetation, usually fruit. The day geckos and the New Caledonian Crested Gecko relish fruit.

One of the oddest things about geckos is that they are vocal; geckos can bark, squeak, chirp, growl, and cluck, depending on species and mood. Some geckos, such as the Tokay and its relatives and the barking geckos of the genus *Ptenopus*, use their voice as a mating call. Most geckos have tails that are easily shed when seized by a predator, leaving the would-be gekkovore with a writhing tail, as the gecko itself dashes to safety. The tails of geckos usually grow back quickly, although they often are deformed and dully colored. Another odd similarity found throughout the family (and shared with Eublepharidae) is that females normally lay only two eggs in each clutch. Lastly, there are skeletal similarities that have led scientist to conclude that the geckos all belong together in one family.

TOKAYS AND KIN

One of the most readily available geckos in the pet trade is the Tokay Gecko, *Gekko gecko*. Fortunately, it is also one of the easiest to care for and is one of the prettiest species. Unfortunately, most are very aggressive, sometimes lunging at their keepers during routine changing of the water bowl. Also, most Tokays are wild-caught and suffer from stress, dehydration, over-crowding, and parasites. This species and a few of its close relatives are being captive-bred in increasing numbers, so if you wish to keep one, you should be able to ferret out a captive-bred neonate.

The genus *Gekko* ranges over much of Asia, from India east to the Philippines, Japan, and Indonesia. The Tokay is found throughout much of

Unknown less than a decade ago, Golden Geckos, *Gekko ulikovski*, now are a staple in the pet trade, imported in large numbers from Vietnam. Few are captive-bred so far, however. Photo: A. Both

that range, occurring from eastern India to Sumatra and the Philippines. It has been widely spread by man, so part of its range is a consequence of this. Feral populations are now established in Florida and Hawaii.

Tokays are largish geckos, reaching 10 inches in total length, with a somewhat stocky build. The tail is long and slender. There is some range in color from purple-brown to a washed out blue, but most are bluish gray. Tokays are extensively spotted with red to orange or brownish spots, with some having white spots as well. The eyes are large and are gold in color. Most Tokays are pretty lizards.

These geckos normally dwell in tropical humid forests, living high in the trees. However, they are supremely adaptable to the presence of man. Large numbers can be found in major cities, living in the buildings and the parks and gardens. They gather at porch lights and street lamps at night to feed upon the insects drawn there.

When housing Tokays, use a tall cage with a tight, screened lid. These geckos, along with most of the other climbing species, are lightning-fast escape artists, so be careful when performing tank maintenance. They do best when given a number of climbing branches and some cover, perhaps cholla cactus

or cork bark stood vertically in a few spots in the cage. Live plants are an option as well. They are not fussy when it comes to substrate. Reptile barks, cypress mulch, potting soil, and recycled paper beddings are all adequate.

In nature, Tokays congregate in some numbers, thus in a large cage several can be housed together. Allow about three gallons of space for each individual and add extra hiding areas and climbing materials. Males tend to fight ferociously, so house only one per enclosure unless using very large (100+ gallons) cages. Males can be identified by their hemipenial bulges, femoral pores, and larger heads.

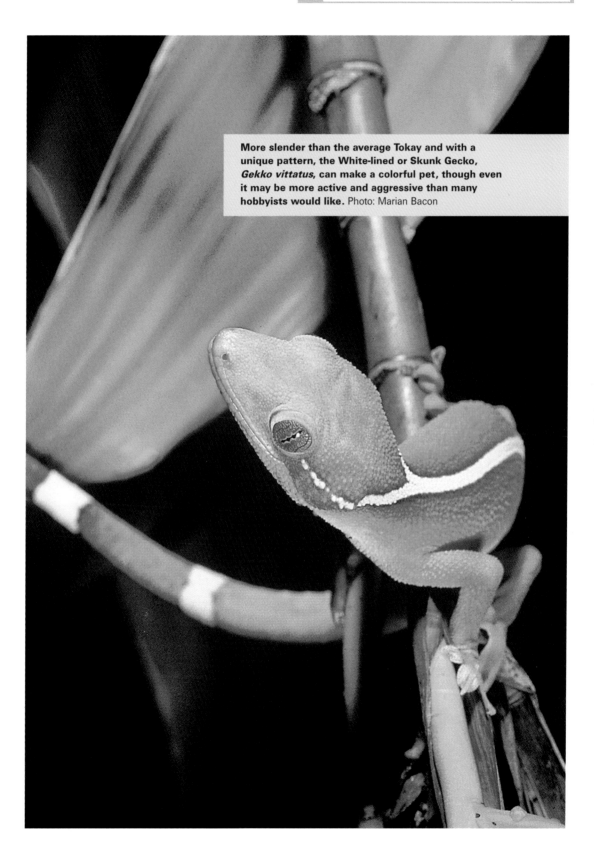

More slender than the average Tokay and with a unique pattern, the White-lined or Skunk Gecko, *Gekko vittatus*, can make a colorful pet, though even it may be more active and aggressive than many hobbyists would like. Photo: Marian Bacon

Tokays are strictly nocturnal and so do not need any special lighting. They do need some heat, preferring temperatures that range from 75 to 88F. This temperature can be maintained with night bulbs and ceramic heaters or by placing the cage in a warm room. Humidity is important with these lizards. The cage should be misted two or three times daily. Not only do they need the air humidity to thrive, but they normally only drink from the droplets formed during the misting. Some, however, learn to drink from a water bowl. Occasionally wetting down the substrate and keeping some live plants in the cage will help keep the humidity up in the acceptable range of 60 to 80%. Tokays should be fed a variety of nutritious insects that are vitamin dusted every third feeding or so. Tokays are large enough to eat newborn mice, should you desire to offer them.

Breeding of Tokays can occur anytime of the year but most commonly takes place when the lizards are given wet and dry seasons. Tokays and many other species of geckos often are called egg-gluers by hobbyists. This refers to the egg-laying behavior of the females. When she lays her eggs, she produces a mucus-like substance and uses this to glue the eggs in a secluded place. Once the glue dries, it is almost impossible to move the eggs without destroying them. If she chooses a plant leaf or piece of bark, move the whole structure to an incubator set to hold a temperature of 82 to 85F with moderate humidity. If she has glued the eggs to the tank glass, you will have to incubate them right where they are. To do this, take a small container and poke a few tiny holes in it. Then tape this over the eggs without touching them. Have some humidifying substrate, such as moistened paper towels or sphagnum moss, in the container, but do not let it contact the eggs. This little chamber will serve as an *in situ* incubator. Check the moisture content of the substrate periodically.

A few other Tokay relatives are rather common in the hobby and can be kept in identical setups. One of these is the Golden Gecko, *G. ulikovski*, hailing from Vietnam and perhaps the surrounding countries. A well-colored individual is pale brown with honey-colored to dull yellow patches across the back. The color is especially vibrant in males. Many are much more brown, which I attribute to the stress of capture, transport, and inadequate housing. They reach a length of about 9 inches. The White-lined or Skunk Gecko, *G. vittatus*, is a greenish lizard with a bright white line down its spine. The line forks at the head and becomes isolated spots on the tail. They reach a size of 10 inches but are much more

Madagascan Giant Day Geckos, *Phelsuma madagascariensis grandis*, may be a foot long and of a uniformly bright green color. Probably the most easily found day gecko, the cheapest, and one of the most colorful, it can serve as a great introduction to the other, more difficult, species of the genus. Photo: Marian Bacon

slender than a Tokay. Their range includes islands from Indonesia to the Solomons. Not as closely related to the Tokay as the other two but requiring very similar care are the flying geckos, *Ptychozoon*. These geckos bear flaps of skin between their legs and toes and along the tail that allow them to glide between trees for short distances. They prefer taller setups than Tokays. Flying geckos are found from Burma to Indonesia north to the Philippines.

DAY GECKOS

Madagascar is home to most of the approximately 60 species of day geckos, genus *Phelsuma*. These geckos are renowned for their splendid colors and diurnal (day-active) behavior. A few species are common in the hobby, a few others are well-represented, and still more are rarely or never seen.

Although most species of *Phelsuma* are found on Madagascar, some occur in

eastern Africa, the Seychelles, the Andamans, Mauritius, Reunion, and few other Indian Ocean islands. One of the most common and most beautiful species, the Gold-dust Day Gecko (*P. laticauda*), is now established and apparently thriving on Hawaii.

For the most part, day geckos are small, averaging about 4 to 6 inches; a few species are smaller and few are larger. The largest, the Madagascar Giant Day Gecko (*P. madagascariensis grandis*), may reach a length of up to a foot and is one of the most popular species in the hobby. Day geckos have uniform granular scales with no enlarged tubercles. Most species are green in color with red, orange, yellow, and sometimes blue markings. Red elongated blotches on the back with red bars on the head are common markings in this genus. Most species are active, arboreal dwellers of tropical humid forests and do not adapt well to other conditions. They are perhaps

best thought of as omnivores, for along with insects day geckos eat substantial quantities of fruit, sap, pollen, and nectar.

Day geckos do not make good choices for the first-time lizard keeper; they are a little too exacting in their requirements. However, once you have kept a few lizards successfully, day geckos make beautiful, keepable, breedable additions to the collection. There is a range in hardiness among the species, with some being suitable only for the *Phelsuma* specialist.

Provide your day geckos with a tall cage; hexagonal fish tanks work very well if you can buy or make a secure screen top. Potting soil makes the best substrate, but reptile barks, cypress mulch, peat moss, and recycled paper bedding are acceptable. The decorations should provide the lizards with opportunities to climb, bask, and hide. Live plants, especially *Sansevieria* and *Dracaena*, and bamboo stalks are highly recommended. Also include some horizontally oriented perches; these geckos love to bask. Day geckos need high humidity, warm temperatures, and good lighting. Use at least one full-spectrum fluorescent light along with an incandescent heat lamp. Temperatures should range from 80 to 90F, dropping to about 70 or 73F at night. Some species require higher or lower humidity than the others. Most of the ones common to the hobby can be kept at 70% relative humidity. Frequent misting is necessary, as most of these animals will not drink water from a bowl. Like Tokays,

The last decade has seen great improvements in our understanding of how to keep and breed day geckos, with several species bred on a regular basis. Young specimens, such as this hatchling *Phelsuma madagascariensis boehmi*, may have patterns much different from those of adults. Photo: R. D. Bartlett

The Gold-dust Day Gecko, *Phelsuma laticauda*, is one of the most attractive species of the genus and is fairly easily available as captive-bred young. Day geckos readily shed their tails and regrow them, and their thin skin is subject to tearing if mishandled. Photo: R. D. Bartlett

males fight and should be kept one to a cage. Two or three females can share an enclosure with a male. Males are determined by the presence of hemipenial bulges and femoral pores. Adult females often develop large sacks under the chin, thought to be reservoirs of calcium needed for egg-laying.

Day geckos will eat all of the standard insect fare, allowing for size. They must be fed daily as they have relatively high metabolisms. It appears that these geckos have rather high calcium requirements, so their feeder insects should be vitamin/ mineral dusted every other day for adults and once every other meal for hatchlings and young. Many keepers place small dishes of powdered calcium carbonate in the cage, allowing the geckos to ingest calcium as they feel the need. Additionally, day geckos consume large portions of fruit and other plant matter. A dish of fresh mashed fruit should be provided at least every other day. The fruit can be mixed with honey, bee pollen, nectar mix manufactured for lories, and fruit baby foods. The best fruits to use are the most nutritious ones, which include mango, papaya, kiwi, melons, peaches, and raspberries. My Gold-dust Day Geckos seemed especially fond of a mixture of mashed bananas, peaches, and honey. Some keepers give small dishes of fruit juices occasionally, and the day geckos lap them up. Vitamin and mineral supplements can be mixed into the fruit.

Breeding day geckos is not always easy. The eggs are small and fragile, and some species are egg-gluers. Also, some species lay their eggs in plant leaf axils, hollow pieces of bamboo, or other inconvenient (for the keeper) spots. If you choose to breed day geckos, find out as much as you can about the species you choose to work with from books and experienced breeders. This section can only present the most general information.

For breeding, group cages with one male and two to four females work the best. Day geckos generally will breed

Once presumed to be extinct, *Rhacodactylus ciliatus*, the New Caledonian Crested Gecko, has made a remarkable "recovery" to become one of the most interesting captive-bred geckos in the hobby today. The large size and generally brownish colors are not for everyone, but the species has many fans.
Photo: Marian Bacon

and lay eggs many times per year if kept in excellent conditions. Some females can lay a clutch of two eggs every three weeks for months at a time. The metabolic strain on such females is considerable. It is advisable that you rotate females out of the group cage after three or four clutches, giving them a month or two of rest with increased calcium in the diet before allowing them to breed again.

You can sometimes trick your females into laying eggs in a convenient place. One way to do this is to have in the cage some easily removed hollow bamboo pieces that have a little moist substrate in the bottom. This works best when the pieces are elevated. When the female lays her eggs in the bamboo, you can remove it to the incubator. The eggs of most day geckos require temperatures of 82F and a relative humidity of 75% to develop and hatch successfully. This takes roughly 50 days. The hatchlings are tiny and will

need plenty of small insect prey, such as fruitflies, pinhead crickets, and springtails. Feed hatchlings twice daily.

NEW CALEDONIAN GECKOS

Several species of large, interesting, and hardy geckos from the tiny island of New Caledonia have made a splash in the hobby of late. These arboreal, nocturnal lizards all belong to the genus *Rhacodactylus*. The most popular of these is the New Caledonian Crested Gecko, *R. ciliatus*. These are being bred in growing numbers, although they are still not typical pet store animals. Some eye-catching color morphs of this animal have become available, further cementing their popularity. They can grow to be just over 10 inches and are heavy-bodied and large headed. Over each eye and continuing down the dorsum is a crest of spiny scales that give the geckos their name. Cresteds can become rather tame and take to gentle handling.

Rhacodactylus leachianus, the New Caledonian Giant Gecko, is the titan of the gecko world. It is the largest living species, reaching a length of just over 14 inches. It has a very short tail and wrinkled skin. The lichenate markings on the brown to greenish background can be quite beautiful. This animal is still a rarity, fetching high prices.

The New Caledonian Rough-snouted Gecko, *R. trachyrhynchus*, reaches a length of nearly 12 inches. It is generally gray to olive in color and is unique in the genus in that it bears live young. This species is not as rare in the hobby as *R. leachianus* but is more uncommon than *R. ciliatus*

The geckos of this genus favor tall terrariums with plenty of hiding spaces. They like temperatures no hotter than about 85F, with night temperatures dropping to 65F. Humidity should be moderate. They eat invertebrates and small vertebrates as well as large quantities of fruit. Some keepers have had success getting *R. ciliatus* to eat turkey and chicken baby food. Males fight viciously with each other, but male-male combat may be key to breeding in some situations. *R. ciliatus* will breed most of the year without any cycling.

LEOPARD GECKOS—NOT ORDINARY GECKOS

One of the most available and highly recommended lizard pets is the Leopard Gecko, *Eublepharis macularius*. These are fairly small, easily cared for, docile, and commonly captive-bred lizards. Thus, they have all the

Rhacodactylus leachianus, the New Caledonian Giant Gecko, appears to be the largest living gecko, sometimes exceeding a foot in length. The heavy body and loose skin give it a unique appeal, as does its generally gentle personality. Photo: R. D. Bartlett

requirements of a good pet.

Despite their common name and many features of their biology, Leopard Geckos are not true geckos. They belong to a closely related family of lizards called Eublepharidae. The easiest way to tell eublepharids from true geckos is to look at the eyes. No true gecko has eyelids, while all of the eublepharids do—yes, Leopard Geckos can blink. For this reason, the eublepharids are often called eyelid geckos.

Leopard Geckos are native to southwestern Asia, specifically northwestern India, Pakistan, and Afghanistan. They are found in sandy to rocky deserts and scrubland. During the day, they hide in their burrows, emerging at night to stalk their invertebrate prey.

As befits their name, Leopard Geckos are yellowish animals with darker spots. The spots can be brown to purple to black and sometimes are arranged in loose bands across the back. The tails of these lizards are whitish to pale purple to gray with dark spots. The trend has been to selectively breed Leopards for interesting colors and patterns, so there are varieties of these animals that bear little resemblance to the normal, wild morph. Some are solid yellow, some have orange background colors, some have the spots elongated into stripes. Albinos have recently been bred in large numbers.

Juveniles have rather different patterns from the adults. They are not at all spotted, instead being yellow with two or three large brown

Normal Leopard Geckos, *Eublepharis macularius*, are yellowish tan with darker spots when adult. For years breeders have been increasing the contrast of the colors while reducing the number of dark spots.
Photo: J. C. Tyson

bands across the body. The top of the head is solid dark brown with a white semicircle just over the nape. The tail is brightly banded in black and white. The eyes of hatchlings and adults are normally a brownish gold.

Leopards make good pets in part because they are small enough to be housed in an average fish tank but large enough to be handled gently. An adult Leopard may reach 10 inches but is usually somewhat smaller. The body is stocky and cylindrical, as is the tail. Their legs are somewhat spindly, but they are strong enough to do some climbing. They have warty skin. Adult Leopards normally have calm demeanors, tolerating gentle handling. Babies may be more nervous and feisty, but they generally settle down. Leopard Geckos live long lives when properly cared for; lifespans of 25 years are not unheard of.

Leopard Geckos have proven themselves adaptable to many terrarium conditions over the years, and their hardiness has been a major factor in their ever-growing popularity. They do well in groups, so long as only one male is included (males have prominent hemipenial bulges and pre-anal pores). A pair can be kept in a 10-gallon tank; five will live happily in a 20. Any number of substrates will work: sand, reptile bark, newspaper, cypress mulch, recycled paper bedding. They do not require very frequent cleaning, although feces should be removed as soon as noted and the entire bedding replaced as needed. A gradient ranging from 75 to 85F is perfect, with drops into the 60s at night acceptable. Being nocturnal, Leopard Geckos do not need full-spectrum lighting. The cage should be dry, but a moist retreat is necessary. A food storage container half-filled with moist sphagnum or vermiculite with an access hole cut into the lid works well. Other shelters should be available. Although the geckos may den together, having at least one shelter per animal is recommended. When you notice that your gecko is in the process of shedding its skin, misting the cage lightly once a day is good husbandry. Like many true geckos, Leopard Geckos often eat their shed skins. Because of their small size and adaptable natures, Leopard Geckos are perfect candidates for naturalistic desert terrariums with live plants.

Leopard Geckos eat the normal insect fare. They have fairly slow metabolisms, so adults should be fed every other day. Hatchlings and juveniles should be fed daily, with vitamin and mineral supplementation provided at every to every other feeding. Adults should be given supplements every second or third feeding. Females that are actively producing eggs should be given supplements with every feeding. Some Leopard Geckos eagerly consume fruit and/or honey, which can be given as a treat. Peach and banana baby foods seem especially popular with Leopards.

One of the great things about Leopard Geckos is that often the keeper need not do anything beyond the normal maintenance to obtain eggs. The eggs will need some care, but Leopard Geckos generally breed without cooling periods or cycling. If your group does not, then you should provide temperature cycling. Leopard Geckos breed most reliably when kept in a harem-type setup, one male with two to six females.

A moistened hidebox will double as an egg-laying site. Like true geckos, female Leopards lay clutches of two eggs. A female kept in excellent condition may lay up to eight clutches a year, but three to five clutches is a more normal number. The clutches are laid roughly three to four weeks apart, with the first one being laid about five weeks after mating.

The eggs should be incubated on damp vermiculite in a humid incubator. Leopard Geckos exhibit a phenomenon called

Selective breeding and luck have led to the development of "designer" Leopard Geckos with bright yellow to orange colors and few or no markings on the back. Albinos, lutinos, and other variants also are being bred, often selling at very high prices. Photo: G. & C. Merker

The Fat-tailed Gecko, *Hemitheconyx caudicinctus*, of western Africa often is confused with the Leopard and can be kept much like that species. Wild-type specimens are tan with broad brown saddles. Photo: A. Both

temperature-dependent sex determination (TSD), meaning that the sex of the babies is determined by the incubation temperature (this is also found in some other lizards, turtles, and crocodilians). If the eggs are incubated at 85F, the ratio of males to females will be about 1:1. At 80F, nearly all of the hatchlings will be female. At about 90F, nearly all will be male. The eggs hatch in five to ten weeks.

OTHER EYELIDS

A number of the other eyelid geckos occur in the pet trade. The most commonly seen of these is the Fat-tailed Gecko, *Hemitheconyx caudicinctus*, a lizard nearly as popular as the Leopard Gecko. Occurring abundantly in western Africa, Fat-tails prefer conditions slightly warmer and slightly more humid than Leopards, but their care is otherwise identical. Fat-tails are found in two naturally occurring varieties, a banded and a striped morph. Both animals are basically brown. The banded ones have bands of dark brown and lighter brown occurring down the length of

The natural tendency for some Fat-tails to have a white dorsal stripe has been used by breeders to produce colorful striped morph Fat-tails. Selective breeding also is brightening the color of the back in this species. Photo: R. D. Bartlett

Hatchling Texas Banded Geckos, *Coleonyx brevis*, are brightly banded, while adults will develop more of a spotted pattern. This species usually is seen as wild-caught specimens. Photo: G. & C. Merker

they are ideal for housing in beautiful natural terraria. Two species, *C. mitratus* and *C. elegans,* are captive-bred in growing numbers. Banded geckos should be housed in dry terraria with moistened hideboxes. Temperatures for Leopard Geckos are fine for bandeds. *C. mitratus* prefers slightly higher humidity.

The strange eyelid geckos of the genus *Goniurosaurus* remain rare and expensive, but some specialists are breeding them. They are called cave geckos, tiger geckos, or demonic geckos. They resemble Leopard Geckos but are very slender, with spindly, stick-like legs. Their eyes are orange to blood red and the banded pattern is brown, purple, rusty, and black. The taxonomy of this group is a mess, and it is not certain which species are in the hobby. They are found in China, Hainan, the Ryukyus, and Vietnam. They are best kept moderately warm and humid.

the body. The bands may be outlined in white. The striped animals have more indistinct bands and bear a bright white stripe from the top of the head down the back and onto the tail. Like Leopards, Fat-tails are docile and hardy pets. Recently, leucistic Fat-tails have been produced; these are attractive animals clad in off-white and pale peach.

North America has a few species of eublepharids commonly called banded geckos and assigned to the genus *Coleonyx*. They are smaller, paler, and more slender than Leopard Geckos but otherwise look similar. Because of their smaller size and somewhat nervous disposition, banded geckos are best not handled. However,

Though still expensive, Oriental leopard geckos, here represented by the recently described *Goniurosaurus luii*, the Chinese Leopard Gecko, are being bred in captivity in fair numbers today and are becoming more available to the gecko specialist. Photo: R. D. Bartlett

DESERT DRAGONS: BEARDED DRAGONS AND OTHERS

BEARDED DRAGONS

One of the most popular lizards in the reptile hobby today is the Inland Bearded Dragon, *Pogona vitticeps*. This Australian native has moved from being an obscure rarity to a staple of the reptile trade in a span of less than six years. A number of factors are involved with this transformation, but perhaps the biggest contributor is their personality. Most Beardies are docile, even friendly lizards that seem to develop more of a bond with their owners than almost any other lizard. On top of this they are hardy, of reasonable size, prolific, and active.

The Inland Bearded Dragon comes from the interior deserts of Australia. It is a member of the family Agamidae, which includes the Green Water Dragon, *Physignathus cocincinus*, and the uromastyx lizards, *Uromastyx* spp. (also called spiny-tails and mastigures). Australia does not allow export of its wildlife, so all Bearded Dragons in the hobby are captive-bred, resulting in mostly healthy, well-adapted offspring being offered for sale at shows and stores.

The Bearded Dragon is a lizard of moderate size. The males may be close to 2 feet in length, while females tend to be around 18 inches long. They are depressed in shape with oval bodies and large,

wedge-shaped heads. The tail makes up about 50% of the length. The edges of the head and body bear conical, spiny scales that are more or less flexible and do not hurt when handling a lizard.

Under the chin there are rows of longish, overlapping scales. When the dragon is frightened or angry, it will inflate this area, creating a spiny beard. This greatly enlarges the size of the animal, hopefully driving off potential predators and rivals. When performing this display, the beard turns jet black and the dragon opens its mouth revealing the bright yellow lining. Combined with hissing and lunging, Beardies have an impressive display.

Bearded Dragons somewhat resemble the swifts, *Sceloporus*, and horned lizards, *Phrynosoma*, of North America and live in similar habitats. Beardies live in hot, arid habitats, from true deserts to dry forests. They climb extensively if there are rocks and trees in their locality. Additionally, they dig large burrows and shelter within them. A good portion of their time is spent basking in the sun. In some areas they are inactive seasonally, retreating to their burrows in winter. In their habitat, they eat whatever animals they can overpower and a large amount of vegetation.

Recently, some nice color varieties of Bearded Dragons have been developed, including specimens that are orange, white, red, red-headed, and yellow. These are more expensive more expensive, in most cases, than the tan natural specimens.

Bearded Dragons are easy lizards to keep, provided their needs are met. One of those needs is space. These are mid-sized, active lizards. Give them as much space as you can, with a 55-gallon tank being considered the minimum size enclosure for one adult dragon. Another need is heat. These lizards like hot temperatures. Use heat lights and heat pads to provide a thermal gradient from 80 to 95F. An incandescent basking light must be provided to give the Beardies a spot where the temperature reaches at least 105F. The best way to do this is to angle a branch up near the light. Beardies like to bask elevated above the ground. Full-spectrum lighting in a necessity. Although one full-spectrum bulb appears to be adequate, two or more will make for more active, brighter colored, healthier Beardies.

Sand and cactus soil make good substrates, but recycled paper bedding and potting soil could also be used. Keep the substrate dry and clean it frequently (these are high-metabolism lizards). The substrate should be deep enough to allow for burrowing or hideboxes should be provided. Climbing branches are recommended. Beardies get along well in groups if there is enough space and you keep a close eye on the colony. Large males will dominate smaller ones, and males may keep females from getting adequate food and heat. If this seems to happen in your group, move the subordinate animals to their own cages. Males are larger, have larger femoral pores, and have bulkier heads than females. Some have visible hemipenial bulges, but many do not.

Feeding Beardies normally is easy. They eat anything that moves and many things that do not. The staple diet should be crickets, with other insects and mice for variety. They also eat great quantities of leafy greens, corn, beans, squash, flowers, fruits, and other vegetation. These should be offered every other day, with insects being offered daily. Although Beardies have a high metabolism and need a lot of food, they are prone to obesity in captivity, so watch your dragon's weight. Insects should be dusted with vitamins and minerals two or three times weekly. When feeding hatchlings and juveniles you *must* be sure the food is small enough. If the prey is too large, the lizards can become paralyzed after eating it—this also happens when mealworms are fed to juveniles. If the prey is longer than one-third to one-half the width of the dragon's head, it is too big. Once the dragon is about four months old, it is big enough to eat larger prey and mealworms without harm. During the first four months, feed your dragons twice daily and supplement the insects once a day. If housing baby dragons in groups, you should feed vegetables to them every day. This seems to prevent them from nipping off each other's toes, tails, and feet, which is likely to happen otherwise.

Bearded Dragons breed at approximately two years of age but may breed at as young an age as 15 months.

Color varieties now are being selectively bred in the Inland Bearded Dragon, but unfortunately bright colors often develop only in adults. This hatchling Sandfire® Gold Phase Beardie shows only a hint of the brighter colors to come as it matures. Photo: G. & C. Merker

The Inland Bearded Dragon, *Pogona vitticeps*, has come from relative obscurity to become one of the most common captive-bred lizards in the terrarium in just five or six years.
Photo: Marian Bacon

Temperature and light cycling is helpful, but in many cases Bearded Dragons have fertile matings without these manipulations. Females lay their eggs about six weeks after mating. A litter pan filled with semi-moist vermiculite, sand, or cactus soil makes a fine nesting box. Beardies like to dig fairly deep nests, so use a large enough litter pan. From 12 to 24 eggs are laid in a clutch, but there may be fewer or a few more. The eggs should be moved to an incubator with high humidity and a temperature of 83 to 85F. They hatch in 55 to 60 days. Females will lay from one to four clutches yearly.

FRILLED DRAGONS

Another denizen of the Land Down Under, Frilled Dragons, *Chlamydosaurus kingi*, can be kept in similar setups as Bearded Dragons and, in room-sized enclosures, can even be housed with them. Frilled Dragons are a bit rare in the hobby but have become more common and less expensive in recent years due to more captive-breeding. Like the Bearded Dragons, Frilled Dragons are members of the family Agamidae.

Frilleds are variable lizards, being colored from olive through gray to black. There often is light banding on the tail and speckles or spots on the flanks. The frill itself may be yellow, black, burnt orange, or any similar shade. Males have slightly larger frills, which can measure as much as a foot across when the animal is engaged in a threat display. A Frilled Dragon may grow to a length of roughly 30 inches. Two-thirds of this will be the tail, which is slender and whip-like. Frilleds are active, nimble, alert animals. They are more nervous than a Beardie, but most hatchlings will become used to handling with time.

There are not many differences between the housing of Frilleds and the housing of Beardies. Frilleds

Frilled Dragons, *Chlamydosaurus kingi*, are not remarkably colorful, can be very difficult to handle, and are bred in just fair numbers, but their incredible neck frill makes them one of the most memorable of all the lizards. Photo: Dr. Z. Takacs

Because of their exceptionally high temperature requirements along with a need for low humidity, spiny-tailed agamids or uros make difficult lizards to maintain in captivity. However, the persistence of a few breeders has paid off, and today several species, including *Uromastyx maliensis*, are available as captive-breds, though still expensive. Photo: R. D. Bartlett

usually do not burrow, so there is no need for a deep substrate; they tend not to use hideboxes either. Climbing branches are an absolute necessity, as these lizards spend much of their time up in branches.

Feed Frilled Dragons insects daily. They normally do not eat plant matter, and they are best regarded as insectivore/carnivores. Obesity generally is not a problem with these lizards. Frilleds drink a lot and should be given the opportunity to soak every once in a while.

Breeding Frilleds normally requires temperature and light cycling. Their clutches number from 8 to 15 eggs, and females may lay up to three clutches a year. Incubate eggs as for Bearded Dragons.

UROS

For the lover of desert lizards who wants one of the tamest lizards imaginable, a uromastyx is the perfect choice. These arid-living agamids occur in Africa, Arabia, and western Asia and are personable, docile pets. Right now, most uros in the hobby are wild-caught, but the breeding of several species is increasing.

The genus *Uromastyx* contains at least 14 species, all inhabiting desert and semi-desert habitats. Several species are present in the hobby in fair numbers, but most are rarely or never seen. Only the Mali and Moroccan Spiny-tails (*U. maliensis* and *U. acanthinurus*, respectively) can be called somewhat

common in the hobby. Uros are medium to large, depressed lizards. They have wrinkled skin and fine scales. On the tails of many species the scales are raised into spines or spikes. The spiny tail makes a good weapon for these mostly inoffensive animals. In color, uros range from the drab gray of the Egyptian Uromastyx, *U. aegypticus*, to the technicolor dreamcoat of the Ornate Uromastyx, *U. ornatus*. Ornates are one of the smaller species, rarely reaching a length greater than 12 inches, while the Egyptian is the largest species, measuring from 24 to 30 inches. All four of the above-mentioned species are bred in small numbers by hobbyists.

Terrariums for uros must be large and provide for their need to burrow. A soil or sand substrate is best. Hideboxes can be buried beneath the substrate with a PVC tube leading to the surface, thus providing your lizard with an artificial burrow. Some keepers have had success using a two-level cage. Humidity must be kept very low, so it might be best to not offer these lizards a water bowl; they will get their water from their food. Temperatures should range from 85 to 95F, with a basking site that reaches at least 110 degrees. At night, a drastic drop to 70 or 75F is recommended.

These are vegetarian lizards, although many will gladly consume crickets and other insects, especially when young. However, animal protein is probably not very good for their metabolism, so insects are best used as an occasional treat. Leafy greens should be the cornerstone of the diet, just as with a Green Iguana, *Iguana iguana*. Uros seem to love flowers; offer dandelions, hibiscus, roses, nasturtiums, and clovers when available. Beans, corn, and small birdseed should be included in the diet roughly every third or fourth feeding. Uros can be fed daily to every other day.

Cycling seems to stimulate breeding in these lizards. Uromastyx are not considered easy lizards to breed, and most eggs do not make it through incubation. If you wish to breed these wonderful lizards, you will need to consult successful breeders, read a lot, and experiment.

COLLARED LIZARDS

Shifting out of Agamidae and from the Old World to the New, one finds some other lizards that are suitable for keeping in conditions similar to those for Bearded Dragons. The several species of the genus *Crotaphytus*, collectively known as the collared lizards and residing in the family Crotaphytidae, will thrive in such a captive habitat.

Collared lizards roam North America from Missouri to California, north to Idaho and south into Mexico. They earn their name from the black and

Most collared lizards seen in the shops are wild-caught and greatly stressed. This captive-bred juvenile *Crotaphytus collaris* shows what the species really should look like—plump and brightly colored. Collared lizards are best kept only if you can get captive-bred specimens. Photo: G. & C. Merker

white collar that adorns the neck of most of the species and subspecies. Males generally have more complete and distinct collars than females. Coloration varies by species, subspecies, population, and individual. Some have bright green bodies with yellow heads, while others are very dull tan and gray. Males tend to be more brilliantly colored than females. Collared lizards may grow over a foot in total length, of which more than half is tail. Like Frilleds, collared lizards are active, alert predators that can run bipedally when pressed for speed. In the wild, collareds eat invertebrates and a large number of other lizards.

Collared lizards in the pet trade are usually wild-caught. These poor animals often fail to acclimate, as they have been kept too cool for a long time. There are captive-bred specimens available, however, and the breeding of these fun and interesting lizards should be encouraged through the purchase of the offspring, rather than contributing to the mass carnage that occurs in the collection, shipping, and holding of collareds.

Set up collared lizards like Bearded Dragons, giving them a very warm (over 100F) basking site. The burrows and hideboxes for collared lizards should be kept a little moist, as these lizards tend to be less able to withstand dehydration than uros or Beardies. They should be fed like Bearded Dragons, but collard lizards will take smaller amounts of vegetation. Some collareds refuse plant matter altogether, and many will take the

A gravid female Eastern Collared Lizard, *Crotaphytus collaris*, displays a pattern of bright red spots on the neck and lower sides. This gravidity coloration is characteristic of the entire genus and the related leopard lizards, *Gambelia*, the only genera in the family Crotaphytidae.
Photo: G. & C. Merker

occasional small mouse. These lizards can become rather tame but never become as docile as Beardies and uros.

Collareds require a two- to three-month hibernation at temperatures in the upper 60s as a preparation for breeding. Females lay several large clutches of eggs. Incubate them like the eggs of Bearded Dragons.

BLUE-TONGUED SKINKS

Though many skinks, family Scincidae, like humid forests (including most of the smaller species found in the shops), the Australian blue-tongues, genus *Tiliqua*, generally are associated with deserts and savannas. These usually large (12 to 18 inches), heavy-bodied, short-legged lizards are noted for the fleshy blue tongue that is displayed when a lizard is cornered or attacked. The widely gaping mouth with blue in the center is enough

to turn away many predators, and the hard bite (powered by large jaw muscles and sharp teeth) will take care of most of the others. Several species of *Tiliqua* are widely available as captive-bred specimens, but all are more or less similar in appearance and requirements. They do well at typical room temperatures with a basking light at one end of the terrarium; gravid females (these skinks give birth to living young) will bask much more than average males. Provide a soft bottom of sand or aspen bedding (or a mix), a hidebox for each animal, and a shallow water bowl. These skinks are omnivores to herbivores, taking a wide variety of greens, fruits, vegetables, crickets, waxworms, earthworms, and young mice. Many keepers have had good success with a diet based on a high-grade dog food to which chopped greens and other vegetables

The bright blue tongue is a characteristic of the species of *Tiliqua* and the source of their common name. The orange spots on the side of this specimen mark it as *Tiliqua scincoides intermedia*, the Northern Australian Blue-tongue, one of the more popular species and subspecies of the genus. Photo: S. McKeown

are added. They will learn to take prepared tegu and monitor diets. Long-lived lizards that can produce broods of up to 20 young in some species, their usually subdued colors (brown, yellow, orange) are compensated for by their strongly developed personalities. The currently most available and inexpensive species, the New Guinea Blue-tongue, *Tiliqua gigas*, is perhaps the least colorful of the group and requires a somewhat more humid terrarium than the desert-dwelling Australian *T. scincoides*, the other common species.

Though less colorful than the Australian blue-tongues, the New Guinea Blue-tongue, *Tiliqua gigas*, is a large, personable species that is available at moderate prices. It also has been bred in captivity many times. Photo: R. D. Bartlett

BIG AND BAD: MONITORS AND TEGUS

Although not closely related, monitors and tegus often are thought of together because of their great size. These are the biggest lizards in the hobby. However, in both families (Varanidae for the monitors and Teiidae for the tegus) there are a number of smaller species as well. The giant species remain the most popular with hobbyists, yet some of the small monitor species have seen a recent surge in their popularity. The giants are imported in great numbers at low cost, so they often find themselves in the hands of beginning keepers not ready to handle such large and dangerous pets. The large species of monitors and tegus are best left to experienced keepers.

LARGER MONITORS

Three species of monitor are common in the pet hobby: the Savanna Monitor, the Nile Monitor, and the Water Monitor. These three are all large, powerful lizards. The Savanna Monitor, *Varanus exanthematicus*, is found over much of Sub-Saharan Africa in grassland to somewhat rocky habitat. It is a predominantly gray animal with a boxy head for a monitor. It can reach a length of 4 feet and is heavy-bodied. The tail is a little less than half of the total length. Savannas are known for being quite tamable and intelligent. If handled and given plenty of attention, they become the most tame of the larger lizards. Savannas are very similar to White-throated Monitors, *V. albigularis*. In fact, White-throats formerly were considered to be a subspecies of Savannas. White-throats are more contrastingly colored and reach a slightly greater size. They are not as common as Savannas in the pet shops but are captive-bred more frequently. They cost a few times the price of a Savanna.

The Nile Monitor, *V. niloticus*, also hails from Africa. It is found mainly along waterways throughout

This young Savanna Monitor, *Varanus exanthematicus*, already displays the box-like head and small-spotted coloration of its species. The lack of a well-developed dark stripe from the eye over the neck is one of the characters separating this species from the very similar White-throated Monitor. Photo: A. Both

the Nile drainage system. Hatchlings are brilliant animals, having a black coloration with yellow bands and ocelli. As they age, the contrast fades, but they remain attractive lizards. Niles are more lanky and slender than Savannas. Nile Monitors easily grow to 5 feet in length and may reach 7 feet. Their long tails account for more than half their length. These lizards have earned a reputation for being aggressive and nasty animals; most do not tame down into anything resembling a pet.

Similar to the Nile in appearance, the Water Monitor, *V. salvator* (not to be confused with *V. salvadori*, the rare Crocodile Monitor), is a species of tropical Asian forests. As its common name suggests, it is a rather aquatic lizard, staying close to rivers, ponds, and seashores. The coloration of Water Monitors is nearly identical to that of Nile Monitors but usually slightly duller. The best way to tell the two apart is to look at the nostrils. Water Monitors have their nostrils very near the tip of their snout, while Nile Monitors have their nostrils set closer to their eyes. Also, the tail of a Water Monitor is more compressed and streamlined than that of the Nile. These are one of the largest of all lizards, possibly reaching lengths in excess of 8 feet. Water Monitors usually are docile, once acclimated to captivity.

OTHER MONITORS

Many other monitor species show up in the pet trade on occasion. As of this writing, the small monitors of Australia are all the rage (though of dubious legality), with some being bred in good

Varanus albigularis **is the southern African version of the Savanna Monitor. The scientific and common names both refer to a white throat, but actually juveniles have black throats, a feature retained in adults from the northeastern part of the range. This species is captive-bred in small numbers.** Photo: K. H. Switak

Nile Monitors, *Varanus niloticus*, are found over much of Africa and are very aquatic lizards. This large adult, while retaining the spotted pattern of juveniles, also displays the high crest on the tail typical of the species. This species is too large and aggressive to be kept as a pet. Photo: C. Polich

numbers. The price tags of these interesting, sometimes colorful, and hardy lizards make them unavailable to most hobbyists. However, as more and more are bred, the prices will drop, so look for some to become reasonably priced in the not too distant future.

The most commonly available of the small Australian monitors is the Ridge-tailed Monitor, *V. acanthurus*, also known as the Ackie. This monitor reaches a length of less than 3 feet and is handsomely colored in red-brown with ocellations of tan, white, yellow, or cream. This is an active lizard that needs a large cage with a sand substrate, hiding areas, and climbing materials. It thrives

in high heat (basking temperatures of 120F are recommended, with cooler retreats, of course) and minimal humidity.

Mangrove Monitors, *V. indicus*, of Indonesia, New Guinea, Australia, and the Solomons, are imported in good numbers and not infrequently captive-bred. These are beautiful animals clad in black with yellow spots. They grow rather large, reaching lengths of at least 4 feet; the tail accounts for more than half the length. Mangroves like tall cages with lots of climbing branches and cover. They tend to be a nervous species. Humidity should be rather high. In nature, this species eats a wide variety of prey; tree crabs

and arboreal rodents seem to figure prominently in the diet.

The spectacular Green Tree Monitor, *V. prasinus*, can be kept in conditions similar to the Mangrove. Mist this species frequently, as it may not drink from a water bowl. This high-priced monitor is rare in the hobby. Breeding it is a true event, not even accomplished often in zoos. *V. prasinus* reaches a size of 2.5 to 3 feet, most of which is tail. Its diet should be insects and crustaceans along with the occasional egg and small mouse.

THE TEGUS

The relationships of tegus are in flux, and the species recognized by hobbyists (primarily by color) do not hold up. Here three species of the genus *Tupinambis* are considered to be in the terrarium hobby. (The Blue Tegu is likely to be a fourth, undescribed species.) The Northern Black and White Tegu, *T. teguixin*, is found over northern South America. There is a single scale in front of the eye and the throat has no spots or only tiny ones. This animal occurs in either a black and white or gold and black form. The gold and black morph usually is called the Gold Tegu, but it is the same species. The Southern Black and White Tegu, *T. merianae*, is found along the coast of southern Brazil down to Argentina. It bears two

scales in front of each eye and large spots on the throat. This species is less frequently imported than *T. teguixin*. Neither species is commonly bred in captivity, but breeding does occur here and there. Both of these species commonly reach 4.5 feet in length, occasionally surpassing 5 feet. *T. teguixin* is difficult to tame, but *T. merianae* generally becomes a good pet.

The Red Tegu, *T. rufescens*, is now bred in good numbers and is not generally wild-caught. It lives in the grasslands of central Argentina north to southern Brazil. The males develop extensive rusty red coloration,

while female are more brown. This species is smaller than the other two, not normally surpassing 4 feet in length. It probably is the most docile species. The higher price tag of Red Tegus generally keeps them unavailable to beginning hobbyists.

HOUSING

These giants start out small, easily being housed in 30-gallon tanks. However, generally by the end of their first year of life they will be several feet long and require larger housing. Most monitor/ tegu keepers build their own enclosures. Such endeavors are beyond the scope of this book, but other hobbyists and

The Water Monitor, *Varanus salvator*, is much like an Asian version of the Nile Monitor, with a similar pattern and very aquatic habits. However, its nostril is placed well toward the end of the snout rather than before the eye. Additionally, large specimens often become very tame and can be handled like dogs—though of course with a good degree of caution. Photo: Marian Bacon

The relatively small size (under 3 feet) and brilliant colors assure the Ridge-tailed Monitor, *Varanus acanthurus*, a place in the terrarium hobby as captive-bred specimens become more readily available. Photo: R. Hunziker, courtesy Goanna Ranch

publications can provide a wealth of information. When building a cage, the length should be at least 1.5 times the length of the full-grown lizard and the width equal to the length of the lizard. Height is not as important a parameter as length and width, but giving the lizards some opportunity to climb is recommended.

All of these lizards like it warm. The background air temperatures should range from 78 to 90F. For the monitors, provide a basking spot—one about as big as the entire animal—that reaches a temperature of at least 115F. Tegus should have a basking spot—again as big as the whole lizard—of at least 100F. It is recommend that you provide full-spectrum lighting to these animals, as they bask

heavily in nature, although there is no real evidence that they need it in captivity. Humidity for the Savanna Monitor and the tegus should be moderate. Nile and Water Monitors prefer higher humidity and water basins large enough to immerse themselves completely. Cypress mulch is probably the easiest and least expensive substrate to use with these lizards; newspaper is another economical option. Be vigilant with cleaning, because these lizards generate a lot of waste. Hideboxes are recommended, especially for the tegus.

When keeping lizards of this stature, personal safety is an important concern. Bites from monitors and tegus can cause horrific damage, possibly resulting in loss of

digits, stitches, scarring, and hospitalization. Also remember that they have formidable claws and strong, whipping tails. Even relatively docile specimens should be treated with all due respect. It would be wise to own strong leather gloves, large burlap bags, and professional reptile restraining tools if you plan to keep any of these animals.

FEEDING

The monitors are almost exclusively carnivores. In the wild they eat any prey they can capture. Savannas, despite their size, eat great numbers of invertebrates in the wild, but they still eat almost anything they can catch. Niles and Waters, as would be expected given their aquatic habits, feed heavily on fish, waterfowl, shellfish, and aquatic

A young Ridge-tailed Monitor is a true gem of a lizard. A desert species, it needs high temperatures, low humidity, and a very large cage to grow into a beautiful adult. Photo: S. McKeown

invertebrates. Nile Monitors are major predators of eggs in crocodile nests, which may also be true for Water Monitors. These lizards should be fed a varied and nutritious carnivore diet consisting of rodents, ground turkey, eggs, large invertebrates, and such.

Savanna Monitors often take well to dog and cat food. Prepared diets now are available for these animals, and the lizards often adapt well to them.

The tegus are similar to the monitors in their dietary preferences. However, many, especially *T. merianae*, will eat

substantial quantities of fruit. In the wild, *T. merianae*, may subsist mostly on fallen fruit during the proper season. The best breeding success for this species occurs when there is a generous portion of fruit in the diet. Commercial tegu diets are widely available.

Obesity is a frequent problem in these lizards, especially Savannas. A diet of rodents and small quarters that do not allow exercise usually are the causes. These lizards should be fed small, varied meals daily and given opportunities to exercise.

BREEDING

Of the large monitors and tegus, the only one that is frequently bred in captivity is the Red Tegu. More White-throats are being bred each year, but there is no financial incentive to breed most of the other large monitors and tegus. The wild-caught imports are sold at prices lower than the

Though often imported and sold at low prices, Mangrove Monitors, *Varanus indicus*, are too large and nervous to be handled and thus cannot be recommended for beginners. Photo: P. Freed

amount it would cost a breeder to produce them. Breeding these lizards is fairly difficult, and there is no set formula. There are several tips that can be given, but interested hobbyists will have to seek detailed breeding information from experienced persons and more technical literature.

As with many reptiles, the most reliable way to breed these animals is to provide them with seasonal cycles of temperature and photoperiod. Drop temperatures by ten degrees and limit the basking temperatures to less than 90F. Whether it's the natural sunlight, the feeling of freedom, or other factors is unknown, but large monitors and tegus housed outdoors (in the appropriate climate) tend to breed more reliably than those housed indoors. Indoors or

Expensive and seldom bred in captivity, *Varanus prasinus* remains the "Holy Grail" of many monitor keepers. The bright green coloration (sometimes a pale blue) and slender shape make it perhaps the most elegant monitor. Photo: I. Francais

Northern Black and White Tegus, *Tupinambis teguixin,* are commonly imported but may not make as good a pet as the other common species of the genus. They are noted for an aggressive temperament. Photo: S. McKeown

The Southern Black and White Tegu, *Tupinambis merianae*, was only recently distinguished from the Northern Black and White. Though generally similar, the Southern species is more adaptable, somewhat tamer, and eats much more vegetation than the Northern. Photo: R. D. Bartlett

outdoors, it is best to keep pairs separate, introducing them only when it's time to breed them. Separate them again after they stop mating (assuming they mate at all) and give the female a large nesting box with moistened sand or vermiculite. The eggs should be incubated with high humidity at 86 to 88F.

Though this book obviously is far from comprehensive, I hope that it will serve you as an introduction to the many fascinating lizards that can be kept as enjoyable pets. The number of lizards to be seen in the shops and at shows continues to grow, and what is rare this year may become relatively common next year. Remember to try to get captive-bred specimens if at all possible if you wish to enjoy this hobby to the maximum.

Red Tegus, *Tupinambis rufescens*, have proved very adaptable to captivity and now are bred in good numbers. Though still expensive, these captive-bred Red Tegus may be the best introduction to the group for the enthusiastic hobbyist. Photo: Marian Bacon